EVERYDAY THEOLOGY

WHAT YOU BELIEVE MATTERS

MARY WILEY

LifeWay Press®
Nashville, Tennessee

Published by LifeWay Press® • © 2019 Mary Wiley

ISBN: 978-1-5359-8543-7
Item: 005820373

Dewey decimal classification: 230.6
Subject headings: DOCTRINAL THEOLOGY / BAPTISTS—DOCTRINES / CHRISTIANITY

To order additional copies of this resource, write to LifeWay Church Resources Customer Service; One LifeWay Plaza; Nashville, TN 37234-0113; order online at www.lifeway.com; fax 615.251.5933; phone toll free 800.458.2772; or email orderentry@lifeway.com.

Printed in the United States of America

Adult Ministry Publishing • LifeWay Church Resources • One LifeWay Plaza • Nashville, TN 37234-0152

TABLE OF CONTENTS

ABOUT THE AUTHOR

Mary Wiley lives with her husband and two children in Lebanon, Tennessee, where they attend and serve Fairview Church. She gets to work with words every day as the manager of women's and kid's books marketing at B&H Publishing Group at LifeWay. Mary holds a Master of Arts in Theological Studies and an under-graduate degree in Christian Studies and English. She hosts the *Questions Kids Ask* podcast and loves good coffee, good conversation over chips and salsa, and learning new things. Read more from Mary at marycwiley.com or connect on social media @marycwiley.

INTRODUCTION

WHY STUDY THEOLOGY?

What you believe matters. It matters on the days you make life-altering decisions and on the days that feel numbingly mundane. It drives how you spend your time, your money, and ultimately, your life. Your beliefs determine the lens through which you see the world and how you respond to both blessing and disaster. Your theology shapes your life.

WHAT IS THEOLOGY ANYWAY?

Theology simply means "the study of God and of God's relation to the world."[1] Don't let this fancy word make you feel like you have to be fancy to study it. I'm about as not fancy as it gets. I'm that girl who often brings store-bought cookies to the potluck. And I'm still utterly amazed that God gifted someone with the intelligence to design seat warmers for cars. So, fancy or not, we are in this study together.

Theology centers on who God is and what God has done, is doing, and will do in the world as revealed in Scripture. Embracing a right theology:

- Helps us identify teaching or worldviews that don't align with Scripture;
- Equips us to make decisions based on biblical principles;
- Compels us to honor God with godly behavior;
- Moves us to rightly worship God.

Theology is not about our gaining knowledge; it's about rightly ordering our lives to honor God. He loves us, pursues us, and redeems us "with the precious blood of Christ" (1 Pet. 1:19). We are His sons and daughters, and as children and heirs, we need to know what the essential beliefs of our faith are.

THAT'S WHERE THIS STUDY COMES IN.

Over the next eight weeks, we'll walk through eight essentials of the Christian faith. This is not an exhaustive study on systematic theology; rather, this study will equip you with a biblical foundation upon which your faith can rest and grow.

I'll provide texts and contexts to give you a clear view of each truth as it is presented in the whole story line of Scripture. Hopefully this solidifies each belief in your heart and gives you a passion to study more of God's Word. Working through a particular book is my favorite way to study, but for these eight weeks we'll jump around a lot, so buckle up.

Some of the best spiritual learning takes place in community. That's why a group discussion time is included in each week of this study. Hopefully the group time is a safe space for you to ask hard questions, wrestle together with the truth of these doctrines, and discuss how to speak the truth in love to people who need to hear it.

MY HOPE FOR YOU

We serve a great God who has given us His Word so that we might know Him and what He has done, is doing, and will do. I pray you see Him in every sentence of this study.

I'm praying specifically that learning key truths about God and His Word will:

- Give you an intense desire to know Him more intimately and surrender every aspect of your life to Him.
- Move you to obey Him.
- Equip you to discern, defend, and proclaim the truth.
- Stir up your affection for Him each day.

The more I study, the more I'm reminded that I am finite and know so little of the vastness of God and His work in the world. I pray we will get a glimpse of the depth of His knowledge compared to the lack of our own. I'm trusting He will meet us here on every page and in every discussion. I look forward to hearing what He does in you and through you in this study.

What you believe really does matter.

Mary Wiley

HOW TO USE

PERSONAL BIBLE STUDY

Each week, you'll find five days of personal Bible study—written to help structure your personal time with the Lord, deepen your understanding of an essential truth, and move you to worship.

Each day includes:

- Scripture passage(s) to study and consider.
- Questions to help you examine the Scripture and apply it.
- Two opportunities to assess and apply what you're learning.
- A prayer prompt to focus your conversation with the Lord about what you've learned.
- Key verse(s) to memorize and meditate on. If one verse per day feels like too much, memorize three per week or even one per week. Meditate on the Word. Chew on it. Soak it up. Let it take root and change your heart. A set of printable memory verse cards are available for you at www.LifeWay.com/EverydayTheology.
- At the end of each week is a "Further Study" section for you to list other questions you may have about the week's study.

RESOURCES

Each week contains extra resources to help you dive deeper into that week's essential belief. The resources can also be a reference tool later when you run into a tough question or need a refresher. These are meant to support the five days of study and can be used or skipped as desired.

GROUP TIME GUIDE

Group leaders: A Group Time guide is included at the end of each week to help your group review the previous week's personal study and apply what you've learned. We suggest you begin your session in a large group, and then break into smaller groups for the rest of the discussion time. Make sure to enlist someone from each small group to facilitate their group discussion.

If you are doing the study on your own, complete the Group Time questions to help you process the content.

GLOSSARY OF TERMS

There is a glossary found on pages 218-219 to define terms that may be unfamiliar to you. Words found in the glossary are designated with _**this style**_ in the content.

INTRODUCTORY SESSION (OPTIONAL)

Note to leaders: We suggest you begin the study of _Everyday Theology_ with an introductory session. This will give you an opportunity to distribute the study books to each participant and explain different aspects of the study and what they can expect. Include a time of fellowship for participants to get to know one another. Consider walking through the Introduction (pp. 6-7), highlighting the sections on what theology is and why we should study it.

Feel free to use the following questions to help drive your discussion:

- How would you define _theology_?
- Are you intimidated by the thought of studying theology? Why or why not?
- Why did you choose this study, and what do you hope to get out of it?
- What truths of the Christian faith do you consider to be essential? Why?
- It's highly possible we will disagree at times in this study. How can disagreement be healthy for building a solid biblical theology? How do we need to conduct ourselves during times of disagreement?
- What initial questions do you have about the essential beliefs presented in this study?

  - Scripture
  - God the Father
  - God the Son
  - The Holy Spirit
  - Humanity
  - Salvation
  - The church
  - The end times

Close the session by spending time praying for one another and for the following eight weeks of study. Ask God to give you a hunger for His Word and to transform your heart as you study.

SCRIPTURE

SESSION 1

SCRIPTURE IS AUTHORITATIVE AND TRUE

What we believe about God is foundational to every other belief we hold. God is the object of our faith and worship, the Person in whom and through whom we have life.

If that is the case, then why start with Scripture?

God has revealed Himself to us in two key ways: through Jesus, the Word made flesh (John 1:14), and through His written Word. Through Scripture we learn about God's character and actions (past, present, and future). It also reveals what we are to believe about God and how we should live. Scripture alone is the authoritative source of our theology.

Why should we believe the Bible is true?

There is external evidence that validates the truth of Scripture. This includes noting the way God has sustained Scripture for thousands of years, the amazing reliability of ancient manuscripts that affirm we read what the early church read, and the consistency across all the books of the Bible, even though they were written by many different authors. (See p. 33 for further discussion on external evidence.)

There is also internal evidence, which is what we will focus on today. Scripture has a lot to say about itself, and every word is valuable and true. Our God cannot lie. How beautiful that the God of the universe would come near by gifting us His Word!

Read 2 Timothy 3:10-17. Complete the following from verse 16:

"All Scripture is _____."

"All Scripture is inspired by God and is profitable for teaching, for rebuking, for correcting, for training in righteousness."

2 TIMOTHY 3:16

What do you think "inspired by God" means? And why is it important?

The word translated "inspired by God" or "God-breathed" (NIV) is *theopneustos* in the original Greek. The English Standard Version uses the literal meaning, "breathed out by God."[2]

The Bible is unlike any other book ever written. It originated with God; He breathed His character into it.[3] But how did it come to be written down?

Hold your place in 2 Timothy and flip to 2 Peter 1:20-21. Where did the "prophecy of Scripture" come from?

The Holy Spirit moved in the hearts of the authors who delivered a message from God in *their* own style and personality. He didn't dictate every word to the writers but led them to choose what He intended for every single word. (This concept is called *verbal plenary inspiration*.)[4]

Why is the Bible the ultimate authority?

The authority of any particular instruction flows from the authority of the person giving it. Whether it comes from a parent, coach, friend, boss, or stranger largely impacts how much weight it carries. Scripture is the authority over every person and every aspect of life because it is breathed out by God. Every word is valuable and without mistake. Because of its authority, Scripture is also useful.

In 2 Timothy 3:16, Paul listed four ways God's Word is useful: for teaching, rebuking, correcting, and training in righteousness.

How does Scripture accomplish this work in your life?

What is the ultimate goal of Scripture according to
2 Timothy 3:17? How would you describe this goal in
your own words?

*The Holy Spirit
illuminates God's
Word as we study it
and hear it taught
and proclaimed.*

Scripture instructs us how to live and provides authoritative discipline to help us course correct when we are straying. It doesn't just point out errors; it trains us in holy living so we can be fully equipped to do the work God has called us to in Christ.

If Scripture is to be useful, then it must be understood. This is the work of the Holy Spirit in us. He helps us understand and apply the Word rightly (John 14:26; 16:13-14). This doesn't mean there aren't passages that are difficult to understand. However, there's no secret code needed to unlock Scripture. The Holy Spirit illuminates God's Word as we study it and hear it taught and proclaimed. He helps us grasp its timeless truths and apply them to our everyday lives.

Why do you think Paul talked about difficult times
(2 Tim. 3:1-13) before reminding Timothy of the truth
of God's Word?

Most scholars believe Paul wrote this letter to Timothy from a prison in Rome just before he was martyred under the rule of the emperor Nero.[5] He reminded Timothy that all who follow Christ will be persecuted. Timothy was serving as a pastor in Ephesus—a city saturated with idol worship and a church quick to believe false teaching about myths and the need for strict adherence to the Law.[6] Paul reminded Timothy to stay faithful to God and His Word.

What might people be teaching today, either with their words or the way they live, that is contrary to God's Word?

False teaching still exists today. It might be a call to ignore sin; a promise that trusting Jesus will result in a happy, prosperous life; or an assertion that we need to live our own truth. It's appealing and may even sound right at times, making it harder to identify as false and more dangerous to our hearts. That's why it's important to thoroughly study Scripture and place ourselves under its authority. As we pore over the Word, the Holy Spirit will help us discern truth from lies. A right understanding of Scripture leads to a life of obedience that looks radically different from the world around us.

How might your life be different if God's Word weren't true?

God has come near to us by gifting us His Word. When it comes to the grand narrative of Scripture, there is no "loosely based on a true story." It's all true, which should compel us to obey and worship Him.

BUILDING YOUR THEOLOGY: Summarize in 1–2 sentences the main point of today's study.

LIVING YOUR THEOLOGY: Explain how this truth affects the way you live your life.

PRAY: Ask God to remind you that His will is for you to love and obey Him and His Word. Ask Him to help you rest in this truth.

MEDITATE AND MEMORIZE: 2 Timothy 3:16-17

SCRIPTURE IS ALIVE AND ACTIVE

As Christians, we believe some hard-to-believe things:

- We believe that our God is one God in three Persons.
- We believe God created the world by speaking it into existence.
- We believe God's Son paid for our sin on the cross and was resurrected three days later.
- We believe that the Bible is God's Word, and that His Word is alive. *Alive*, people.

Read Hebrews 4:12-13. List what this passage says is true about God's Word.

To provide some context, the writer of Hebrews spent the bulk of chapter 3 and the first part of chapter 4 discussing entering God's rest. He warned his readers not to turn "away from the living God" (3:12) or be "hardened by sin's deception" (v. 13), but to "hold firmly until the end" (v. 14). He used Psalm 95 to exhort them: "Today, if you hear his voice, do not harden your hearts" (v. 15). He reminded them of how the Israelites failed to enter God's rest (the land of promise) because they rebelled. They heard the "good news" (4:2) but didn't believe it. And only those "who have believed enter the rest" (v. 3). He pleaded with his readers not to suffer this same fate, reminding them that the opportunity to enter God's rest of atonement was still available for those who put their full trust in Christ with enduring faith.

The author of Hebrews made clear that the opportunity to enter that rest is now—*today*. He again referenced Psalm 95 in 4:7, urging readers to hear the voice of God. And he gave a warning in verse 11: "Let us then make every effort to enter that rest, so that no one will fall into the same pattern of disobedience." This urgent, essential message is followed by the statement on the Word of God in verses 12-13.

Write out Hebrews 4:12-13 below.

Note "that this description of God's Word echoes the author's treatment of Psalm 95, with its emphasis on the 'voice' of God that we should 'hear' (95:7). Psalm 95, therefore, forms the basis for the author's comments on 'the word' in Hebrews 4:12-13."[7]

The ancient readers of Hebrews and the current ones—you and I—need to know that Scripture isn't just words on a page; it is the powerful voice of God. The Word won't allow us to fake it or skirt by. It penetrates. It rightly divides. It is powerful to speak, convict, and expose. It can't be taken for granted or disobeyed without consequences. Consider what happened to the Israelites when they disobeyed the voice of God. Scripture speaks authoritatively into our lives, and we cannot push it to the side. We must respond in faith, not with hard hearts.

What do you think it means for Scripture to be living and active?

God's Word is neither dead nor ineffective. It is living because it is the Word of the living God. God's Word is active, meaning that the Holy Spirit is working through it every time we open its pages to help us understand, illuminating it for us.

What does it mean that Scripture is sharper than a double-edged sword?

How is Scripture able to judge the thoughts and intentions of the heart? How have you personally experienced this?

Each verse of Scripture is like a scalpel in the hands of an able surgeon, opening us up and revealing disobedience, calling us to repentance and correction, and thus restoring us to a place of joy and obedience. The sword of God's Word is so sharp that it can penetrate the hardest parts of our hearts and bring our deepest motives and rebellious thoughts into the light. It cuts through both our soul, or, as John Piper says, "the invisible dimension of our life that we are by nature,"[8] and our spirit, or who we are supernaturally in Christ. Scripture shows us our true selves, judging rightly our actions and motives.

The Word is alive and active, working powerfully to accomplish God's purposes in us and through us.

> Read Isaiah 55:8-11. What does it mean that God's Word does not return empty?

Scripture that is spoken, read, studied, and lived will effect change and bring a harvest of righteousness.

God's Word does not go out without producing fruit. Scripture that is spoken, read, studied, and lived will effect change and bring a harvest of righteousness. Like rain and snow that fall in winter, the impact of Scripture may not be immediately seen, but spring will come and the results will be apparent.

However, life only springs from the ground that's been watered, cultivated, and tended. The farmer must be intentional about caring for the fields and the crop. The same is true of our spiritual lives. If I'm not spending time with God in His Word, then I'll lack spiritual fruit. My spiritual life will wither if I'm not consistently seeking the source of my nourishment in His Word.

Too often I allow the busyness of life to replace the still moments with the Lord. I easily allow my to-do list to dictate my every hour rather than taking time to hear from the God who created me and saved me. If I choose to ignore my dependence on God's Word, then I'm saying I can control my own circumstances. I can make my fruit grow.

What excuses do you use for skipping time in God's Word?

If God's Word truly is alive and active, never returning void, then a single minute in it is never wasted, and every verse is useful.

What needs to change in your schedule to prioritize spending time in God's Word?

If God's Word truly is alive and active, never returning void, then a single minute in it is never wasted, and every verse is useful. That's true whether you're folding clothes, sitting on a beach, or being the taxi driver for your children. God's Word has the hope that you need for today.

BUILDING YOUR THEOLOGY: Summarize in 1–2 sentences the main point of today's study.

LIVING YOUR THEOLOGY: Explain how this truth affects the way you live your life.

PRAY: Ask God to help you prioritize time in His Word. Thank Him that it is living and active and reveals the true motivations of your heart.

MEDITATE OR MEMORIZE: Hebrews 4:12

DAY 3

SCRIPTURE IS FOREVER

> Define *forever* in your own words, then write the dictionary definition.

When we use the word *forever*, we're often referring to an annoyance like a long wait at the doctor's office or in the grocery checkout line. But when the Bible says that God's Word endures forever, it means it never passes away, never goes out of style, and remains beneficial throughout all eternity.

God has been sustaining His Word throughout generations, protecting its integrity and its existence despite many attempts to snuff it out. Antiochus Epiphanes, a Seleucid king who ruled in the second century BC, tried to destroy all copies of Scripture during a bloody persecution of the Jews.[9] Then in AD 303, the Roman emperor Diocletian demanded all Scripture be confiscated and destroyed.[10] However, God sustained His Word despite these and other attempts and will continue to do so.

> Read Isaiah 40:8. Draw a healthy flower and blade of grass below. Then draw both plants withered.

I'm no expert gardener, but the life span of both the flower and grass seem very short, as is the life span of everything else on earth. Situations or people may fail us, but God's Word can be trusted. It will not end, and it will not fail. It is not like the grass and the flowers, springing into life for a moment and then fading away. God's Word is always alive and active and true. It will not change, and it will not become irrelevant.

What does it mean to be relevant? Do you believe God's Word is relevant today? Why or why not?

The timeless truth of God's Word continues to resonate in every generation. The Bible is not just some old book written for another people in another time. Although understanding the historical context of Scripture is critical for right interpretation, the Bible is not stuck in history. It applies today. Popular books come and go, but the Bible remains useful for teaching, rebuking, correcting, and training in righteousness.

Read Psalm 119:89-112.

Psalm 119, the longest chapter in the Bible, is devoted to celebrating God's Word. The psalm is an acrostic, composed of twenty-two stanzas with each stanza containing eight verses. Each of the eight verses in a stanza start with the same Hebrew letter. Almost every verse in this psalm contains one of the following words describing God's Word: instruction, decree, precept, statute, command, judgment, promise, and word. You'll often see the word *delight* in the chapter too. (More on delighting in God's Word tomorrow!)

I love that even the structure of this psalm reveals God's character. He is not a God of chaos but of order. This is such an encouragement to my heart, especially when life feels out of control and messy.

Write Psalm 119:89-91 in your own words.

The psalmist praised God for His eternal Word and for His eternal faithfulness.

What will last eternally? List as many items as you can.

The list for what lasts forever is short: God, His Word, and people. That's it. Unfortunately, I tend to become very attached to things that will not last: jobs, relationships, easy seasons of life, financial security. I can become incredibly driven to preserve these at all costs. And every time I do, I uproot God from the throne of my life, replacing Him with one of these lesser gods. I ignore God's eternal Word and choose what I believe will be a better way.

What temporal idol do you most often place on the throne of your heart? How and why do you let that idol drive your life?

Our constant striving to earn more "likes" on the Internet, to achieve some level of success in our work or our personal lives, or to meet some standard of beauty so we might be applauded seems silly in light of forever.

Don't trade the eternal for the temporal. Don't be driven by whatever is in front of you right now. The things of this earth wither and fade. Our constant striving to earn more "likes" on the Internet, to achieve some level of success in our work or our personal lives, or to meet some standard of beauty so we might be applauded seems silly in light of forever. As verse 96 says, there is a limit to perfection. Regardless of how hard we work or the success we achieve, it still pales in comparison to the eternal glory to come. Stay the course.

Read Psalm 119:92. Is that also your testimony? Explain.

Read Psalm 119:97-104. How did the psalmist become so reliant upon God and His Word?

If we love God's Word without loving God, we become full of knowledge but miss life's most vital relationship and the fruit that comes from it, including the salvation of our souls. If we love God without loving God's Word, we don't really know the object of our affection. We may bow to a god we've created in our heads instead of the true God of Scripture. This is dangerous ground. We must love Him and the Word that reveals Him.

> Read Matthew 24:35. What does this say about God and His Word?

Our God is _sovereign,_ and His reign is eternal. Every word of Scripture is true and every promise will be fulfilled. His Word has stood and will stand the test of time. It will go forth and not return void. It will pierce our hearts so that we might know Him and obey Him. That is worthy of worship!

BUILDING YOUR THEOLOGY: Summarize in 1–2 sentences the main point of today's study.

LIVING YOUR THEOLOGY: Explain how this truth affects the way you live your life.

PRAY: Spend time praising God for His Word and His faithfulness to preserve it forever. Thank Him for revealing Himself and the grand story of the gospel of Christ that we might know Him and be with Him forever. Praise Him specifically by praying Psalm 119 as you worship.

MEDITATE AND MEMORIZE: Isaiah 40:8

SCRIPTURE IS WORTHY OF DELIGHT

Read Psalm 1. What characterizes a "happy" or
"blessed" (NIV) man?

Charles Spurgeon described Psalm 1 as the preface psalm, or the
"Psalm of Psalms," because it reveals the intention of the whole
book: "to teach us the way to blessedness, and to warn us of the
sure destruction of sinners."[11]

Psalm 1:2 states that the happy man's "delight is in the
LORD's instruction." What do you think that means?

Throughout the psalms, we see that delighting in God's Word is
central to the life of God's people. Delighting in God's Word means
we hunger for it. We find our spiritual nourishment and fulfillment in
God through His Word. It means allowing Scripture to define who
we are and to direct our paths. We trust the Word of God because
we trust Him. He knows how creation works best because He created it, and we believe He is working all things for our good and His
glory (Rom. 8:28). We can lovingly and without hesitation obey His
Word, knowing that "the LORD watches over the way of the righteous"
(Ps. 1:6). God's Word—both the encouraging and the convicting
verses—is life to those of us who trust Jesus.

Why do you think the psalmist described the happy man as
"a tree planted beside flowing streams" (v. 3)?

The Middle East is a dry, arid place, so lush vegetation isn't the
norm. Yet this tree is the picture of health because of its proximity
to water, which provides life. God's Word is life to us. It is our

nourishment (Matt. 4:4). It is worthy of delight. However, we can't hold it at arm's length, simply giving it a cursory nod of approval. To delight in God's Word means we must take it in.

> What does the happy man do with the Lord's instruction (v. 2b)?

> What does it mean to meditate on Scripture?

To meditate on Scripture means to reflect on it, marinate in it, and consider its truth and how to apply it. Bartholomew Ashwood said it this way: "Meditation chews the cud, and gets the sweetness and nutritive virtue of the Word into the heart and life: this is the way the godly bring forth much fruit."[12]

We are not only to meditate on the Word but also memorize it. The two go hand in hand.

> Read Psalm 119:9-16. Why should we memorize Scripture?

Meditating on and memorizing God's Word helps it to dwell deeply within our hearts, to provide comfort when we're afraid, and to correct us when we've strayed. It helps us identify truth from Satan's lies and becomes a weapon against him when he tempts us, just as it was for Jesus when He was tempted (Matt. 4:1-11). It helps equip us to share the gospel and also to defend our faith.

> Are you currently meditating on and memorizing God's Word? Why or why not? If not, what needs to change for you to begin these important _spiritual disciplines_?

Knowing and loving God's Word is a result of knowing and loving God, and knowing and loving God is a result of knowing and loving God's Word.

> Why does it matter that we see God's Word as worthy of delight rather than just a list of rules to follow or tasks to be completed?

> What might cause us to see God's Word in a negative light instead of celebrating and rejoicing in the freedom and life found within its pages?

The psalmist rejoiced in God's Word, not because it was his duty to obey, but because it was his privilege to do so. We don't normally think of instructions as worthy of delight. Yet rules and instructions are given to protect, guide, and teach.

God's statues are worthy of our delight because they reveal His love for us and His desire that we flourish as His children. Like children with good parents who make good rules (like not eating ice cream for every meal), we can trust the good rules set by our Father just as the psalmist did. Every rebuke, instruction, and promise in Scripture is for our good and is worth treasuring.

> Read Exodus 20:1-2. Why do you think God prefaced the Ten Commandments by reminding Moses of His goodness to His people?

God summoned Moses to Mount Sinai three months after the Israelites left the land of Egypt (Ex. 19:1). They were headed to Canaan, the land God had promised. Before giving Moses the Ten Commandments, God issued a reminder: *I'm the God who loves*

God desires devotion from a love relationship, not dutiful, begrudging compliance.

you. I delivered you. God was defining the heart of obedience He desired—devotion from a love relationship, not dutiful, begrudging compliance. The Israelites complained a lot as they wandered through the wilderness, but we never see them complain about the Law. It was life to them.

However, they could not perfectly obey it, and the continual sacrifices they made to atone for sin were not sufficient. That's why God sent Jesus to be the perfect sacrifice. He didn't come to abolish the Law but to fulfill it, to complete it (Matt. 5:17). By His blood we are now redeemed, declared righteous, and no longer live under the condemnation of the Law (Rom. 3:21-26).

> Why is the Law still important, valuable, and delightful to us?

The grace of Christ we live under now doesn't give us freedom *to* sin but freedom *from* sin. We are no longer slaves to sin but slaves to righteousness, called to walk in holiness and loving obedience (Rom. 6). All of Scripture, including the Law, points the way.

BUILDING YOUR THEOLOGY: Summarize in 1–2 sentences the main point of today's study.

LIVING YOUR THEOLOGY: Explain how this truth affects the way you live your life.

PRAY: Reread Psalm 1, then use it to guide your prayer time today.

MEDITATE AND MEMORIZE: Psalm 1:1-3.

DAY 5

SCRIPTURE IS TO BE LIVED

When I was a teenager, my room was always a mess. I mean, a real mess. My mom would ask me to clean it about seventeen times before reminders turned into threats. Only then would I jam my strewn stuff into my closet or under the bed. You know, cleaning without really cleaning.

I wasn't a doer of the instruction my mom had spoken; I was simply a hearer. Sometimes I fooled myself into thinking I had satisfied her cleanliness requirements. I had the appearance of obedience, but I couldn't deceive my mom forever. She would eventually drop off a pair of shoes in my closet and be welcomed by an avalanche of junk. Similarly, but even more so, God is not deceived by our charade of obedience. Instead, God is concerned with the hearts of His people. His will is that we would love and obey Him in every moment, seen and unseen.

> Read James 1:19-27. Describe a time when you were a hearer and not a doer of God's Word. How might things have been different if you had obeyed?

James, the author of this passage, was the son of Mary and Joseph. He grew up as Jesus' brother and saw Him be a faithful doer of the Word. James wrote this letter to Jewish Christians dispersed throughout Gentile lands, who were experiencing persecution (1:1). It seems that those who were living away from Israel were tempted to adopt the practices of the land in which they were living. By doing so they could fit in, not experience any pushback, and not seem weird to those around them. We can relate, right?

Yet James didn't give them an out to take the easy path and fall in line with the practices of the pagan cultures. Instead, he called them to continue in obedience to the Word.

Review James 1:19-21. What instructions did James give in this passage?

What do you think it means to "humbly receive the implanted word" (v. 21)?

The Letter of James implores us to be eager to hear and obey the message of God. To listen. To practice restraint. David Platt states that we often approach Scripture wanting it to say what we want it to say. He says, "We are not quick to hear and slow to speak but loathe to listen and anxious to argue."[13]

Instead we are to "humbly receive the implanted word" (v. 21). This word planted in us has brought about our new birth and continues to do the work of salvation in us (v. 18). It sanctifies us and leads us to ultimate salvation—the moment when we see Christ. To humbly receive it means we do so with a continually submissive and teachable heart.

Write a one-sentence summary of the illustration James used in verses 22-25.

Based on James 1:22-25, what characterizes a doer of the Word?

God's Word changes our hearts. Therefore, to read, study, and experience God's Word, but then to forget it or live contrary to what we've read would be the opposite of what should be true of us. Instead, James stated that we are to look intently into it and persevere in it (v. 25).

The Word of God is not a sound bite that we acknowledge as a clever thought but then go our way and forget it. No, we must look into it, study it, remember it, and live it. The Word is to be applied, and practiced. We deceive ourselves if we think we can just read it, maybe even study it, but not live by it.

What is the promise to the doer of the Word in verse 25?

We deceive ourselves if we think we can just read it, maybe even study it, but not live by it.

This isn't a promise that all of your dreams will come true if you obey God's Word. It's not a guarantee that you'll never be sick or sad again. But this verse does promise God's blessing for those who walk with Him. That blessing may take different forms, but His greatest blessing is His presence. He is with and within the doer of the Word.

What does it look like to be a hearer of the Word and not a doer? How does that affect your plans and purpose?

It would be much easier to read God's Word and not be required to do anything with it. But James says those who read and listen and yet are not compelled to act deceive themselves into thinking they are obedient servants of the Lord.

Write John 14:15 below. This verse is an if-then statement. Underline the *if* statement. Circle the *then* statement.

Sometimes portraying an outward appearance of obedience isn't difficult. We can do the right things, go to the right places, and say the right things to make people think we know, love, and obey God and His Word. Yet our hearts might be far from Him. Just know, He is not deceived. Instead, He lovingly calls us back again and again to walk in holiness by being doers of His Word.

Being a doer of the Word also means being a pray-er of the Word. We will not perfectly walk in step with Him at all times, but we can ask God to make what we read in Scripture true by praying it back to Him. Praying Scripture also helps us be specific in our praying, gives us the words to say when we are lacking, and helps us maintain the right focus.

Are you currently a doer of the Word? If not, why not? What needs to change for you to walk in obedience to Scripture?

God's Word is not just to be read; it is to be lived.

God's Word reveals who God is and how we can find Him. It shows us His will and ways. It gives guidance, direction, and wisdom. But it is not just to be read; it is to be lived.

BUILDING YOUR THEOLOGY: Summarize in 1–2 sentences the main point of today's study.

LIVING YOUR THEOLOGY: Explain how this truth affects the way you live your life.

PRAY: Ask God to reveal your true status as a doer of the Word. Pray for a humble heart so God can use the implanted Word to do His work in you.

MEDITATE AND MEMORIZE: Psalm 119:105

FURTHER STUDY: What other questions do you have about the Bible?

RESOURCES

HOW TO READ SCRIPTURE

When it comes to reading Scripture, the best advice is to read it often, deeply, and widely. The Bible is a book and should be read as one. <u>Context</u> is incredibly important. Keep an eye on what is going on immediately around the text within the particular book.

Always keep the big story of Scripture in mind as you read, which can be summarized like this:

CREATION

God created all things out of nothing, and everything He created was good. He created man and woman in His image. There was peace.

FALL

The man and woman God created and placed in the garden disobeyed Him. All of creation, including humanity, is now broken by sin and experiencing its consequences.

REDEMPTION

The punishment for sin is death. Yet God, in His infinite kindness, chose to send His Son, Jesus, to pay for sin. He lived the life of sinlessness that we couldn't live and paid the price for sin that we couldn't pay by dying on the cross. He rose again three days later, proving that He had paid for sin and defeated death.

RESTORATION

One day Jesus will return and will judge sin and evil. Sin will be cast out forever, and there will be no sickness, sadness, or death. He will also renew and restore all of creation, and His people will dwell with Him forever.

HOW TO STUDY THE BIBLE

One method of Bible study I recommend is called inductive Bible study. Books have been written on this method, so we won't cover all the bases here, but on the next page is a brief overview.

This method has three major steps:

1. Observation—What does the text say?
2. Interpretation—What does the text mean?
3. Application—What does the text mean for my life?

OBSERVATION
Again, context is vital. Note what comes before the text and what comes after it. Ask as many questions as possible about the text.

INTERPRETATION
Begin by asking who the original hearers were and what the author's original intention was. What was the occasion? What is this text's main point? What problem is being addressed?

APPLICATION
When we understand the context of the passage and what the author intended for the original audience to learn, we can make it actionable. What is this passage asking us to do? How should we live in light of this passage?[14]

TIPS FOR MEMORIZING SCRIPTURE
1. Record yourself reading the verse(s), and then listen back to it as you commute or work around the house.
2. Write it. Journaling the verse or drawing it in a notebook gives the opportunity for tactile learning.
3. Make up a song or search for a recorded song for the passage you are memorizing. Everything is easier to remember when it's set to a tune.
4. Print out cards from LifeWay.com/EverydayTheology or write the verses used in this study on note cards. You can carry them with you for a quick review.
5. Enlist a friend to memorize with you. Text the verses you are memorizing to each other. Then quote them to one another via phone, voice text, or in person each week.

FAQS

How reliable are the ancient manuscripts?
We have more ancient copies of the New Testament manuscripts than any other book. Homer's *Iliad* and *Odyssey* were highly treasured in the ancient Mediterranean world. We have twenty-five hundred total manuscripts between these two works, making them highly reliable.[15] Yet scholars have indexed more than fifty-seven hundred manuscript portions of the New Testament in Greek, making the total number about twenty-five thousand when added to early translations in other ancient languages.[16] God has miraculously sustained His Word since the beginning.

Why are there multiple translations?
Every Bible translation lands on a continuum, ranging from strictly word-for-word translation to strictly thought-for-thought. The word-for-word translation (e.g., NASB) seeks to stay as close to the original word order and grammatical structure of the Hebrew (Old Testament) and Greek (New Testament) texts as possible. A thought-for-thought translation (e.g., NLT) seeks to translate the original intended meanings of the biblical texts. Reading and studying the Bible using multiple translations can help you better understand meanings and concepts. You can quickly access multiple translations online through apps and websites such as *Bible Gateway* and *YouVersion*. When choosing a Bible, select a translation that is easy for you to understand and true to the text.

When were chapter and verse numbers added?
Chapter and verse numbers are not divinely inspired. They were added centuries after these works were written to make it easier to locate a passage being referenced. Chapter and verse numbers were first printed in English in the Geneva translation in 1557.[17] The divisions shouldn't have any bearing on our interpretation of Scripture.

(For more resources about Scripture, go to LifeWay.com/EverdayTheology.)

GROUP TIME

OPEN

Begin your group time with the large group discussing the following questions:

What was the highlight of your week of study?

What was something new you learned this week?

How did this week's study challenge what you believe about Scripture?

REVIEW AND DISCUSS

Break into smaller groups to complete this section. Use the following Scripture passages and questions to review what you learned in your personal Bible study on Scripture.

Read 2 Timothy 3:16-17.
How does this passage speak to the authority of Scripture?

How has the Bible taught, rebuked, corrected, and trained you?

Read Hebrews 4:12.
How would you explain the work of Scripture described here?

How has the Bible been alive and active in your life?

Read Isaiah 40:8.
How does Scripture's eternal quality speak to its trustworthiness?

How have you seen the truth of God's Word stand up over time?

Read Psalm 1:1-3.
How is the Bible worthy of your delight?

What is your current practice for meditating on and memorizing the Word? Why are both disciplines so important to your spiritual life?

Read James 1:22-25.
What does it mean to be a doer and not just a hearer of the Word?

How are you currently looking intently into the Word?

REFLECT AND APPLY
Spend a moment writing your answers to the following questions, then discuss with your small group.

What other questions about Scripture did this week's study raise?

What's your main takeaway from this study on Scripture?

Why does what you believe about Scripture matter?

What will you do this week to seek to cultivate a love and hunger for God's Word?

CLOSE
Determine as a small group to hold each other accountable for reading, studying, meditating on, and memorizing God's Word. Close in prayer, thanking God for His Word and asking Him to give you an insatiable hunger for it.

GOD

SESSION 2

DAY 1

GOD IS THREE IN ONE

God is both able to be known and full of incomprehensible mystery. One of those mysteries is God's triune nature. Our God, the God of the Bible, is one God in three Persons.

I wish I could eloquently and simply explain the mystery of the _Trinity_, but it is impossible. And every analogy used to try and explain it eventually breaks down. (See the Resources section on p. 57.) It seems our attempts to simplify the complexities of God only result in a grander view of His vastness, giving us an opportunity to stand in awe of Him.

Despite the complexity of God's triune personhood, the Trinity isn't a liability to the Christian faith; rather, it sets our faith apart from other world religions. It clarifies our understanding of God's character as we see the unity of the Trinity in its work of creation, salvation, and sanctification. My mind can't quite comprehend all this, but I consider the Trinity to be the most beautiful and foundational truth of our faith.

> Read Deuteronomy 6:4-9. Finish this statement: "The LORD our God, the LORD is _____" (v. 4).

> Skip down to verses 14-15. What do these verses tell us about the culture of the day?

Almost every culture during this time practiced either _polytheism_ (the worship of many gods) or _henotheism_ (the worship of one god but belief in many gods).[18] With this statement in verse 4, God was setting Israel apart from the people they would encounter as they entered the promised land. The declaration of God's oneness doesn't oppose the trinitarian view of God; rather, it is a statement of supremacy, unity, and uniqueness. God is One and there is no other.

God is not powerful over just one aspect of life but all of life.

It was vital for the Israelites to embrace this truth. And to pass it down.

What was Moses' instruction to the people in verses 6-9?

Israel's God, the God we worship, is distinct and <u>transcendent</u>. He is not powerful over just one aspect of life but all of life. He is sovereign, reigning over and in control of all things. He is altogether holy and wholly other. There is none like Him. Yet He is infinitely faithful, making a way for us to be holy before Him through the triune goodness of the Father, Son, and Holy Spirit. This is the delight and distinctiveness of Christianity.

The word *Trinity* is not found in Scripture, but the concept is made clearer as the story line of God's Word progresses.

Read the following passages and record how each reflects the reality and work of the Trinity.

GOD THE FATHER	GOD THE SON	GOD THE HOLY SPIRIT
Genesis 1:1-2		
Matthew 3:16-17		
John 1:1		
2 Corinthians 13:13		
1 Peter 1:2		

These passages point to the Trinity as being active together, each Person coequal with the others in their God-ness. Each Person is eternal (has existed and will exist forever), all-knowing (<u>omniscient</u>), all-powerful (_omnipotent_), ever-present (_omnipresent_), and unchanging. They are perfect in their union, indivisibly sharing in divine perfection, action, and mission. There is no hierarchy with one Person being more powerful or supreme than the other.

Each Person of the Trinity is distinct from the others. The Father is not the Son or Spirit, the Son is not the Spirit or Father, and the Spirit is not the Father or Son. The Father begets the Son, and the Spirit proceeds from the Father and Son. They are unified and distinct—one God—not three gods or three views of one Person.

They also are distinct relationally (as Father, Son, and Spirit) and functionally. "The Father exercises the primary role in creation (working with the Son and the Spirit to create). The Son exercises the primary role in salvation (working with the Father and the Spirit to save). The Holy Spirit exercises the primary role in sanctification (working with the Father and the Son to bring transformation)."[19]

> Read Ephesians 1:3-14. How has God the Father blessed us according to this passage?

> How does each person of the Trinity act in salvation?

God chose us in Him by His eternal plan, sent Jesus the Son to redeem us by shedding His blood, then sealed us for eternity by the Holy Spirit. Without the triune nature of God, our faith would be in vain.

God is love because there is perfect love among the Persons of the Trinity. He displays His love to us through Jesus and pours out His love for us through the Spirit, His presence with us. The Spirit unites us to Christ so that we might delight in the Son, and in that union we might be most delighted in by the Father. Our faith is informed by and hinges upon the truth of the Trinity.

What is one specific way the study today has helped you better understand the Trinity?

What questions remain for you about the Trinity?

To know God is to know Him as the Trinity, and knowing the One we worship helps us rightly talk about, think about, and praise Him.

It's OK to still be a bit baffled about the Trinity. It is a mystery that will not be totally understood this side of eternity. But that doesn't mean we discard it or ignore it. To know God is to know Him as the Trinity, and knowing the One we worship helps us rightly talk about, think about, and praise Him. He is incomprehensible and transcendent and yet close and personal. He is the Father who generates all life, the Son who reveals the Father and saves God's people, and the Spirit who is the Giver of eternal life, comfort, and guidance. Our God is three Persons but one God. He is unlike the false gods others worship. He is beyond what we can think or imagine, and He is good.

BUILDING YOUR THEOLOGY: Summarize today's key truth in 1–2 sentences.

LIVING YOUR THEOLOGY: How does this truth affect the way you live your everyday life?

PRAY: Praise God for being beyond our comprehension and being the one true God. Give thanks for the way each Person of the Trinity has worked in your life.

MEDITATE AND MEMORIZE: Deuteronomy 6:4-5

DAY 2

GOD IS HOLY

How would you describe God's holiness?

God is superior to us in all things, even in the attributes He shares with us. We display a tiny glimpse of His righteousness, purity, and goodness, while He is all these perfectly. *Holiness* is a single word that sums up all of His perfection and superiority.

Read Isaiah 6:1-4. Who saw this vision? Whom did this prophecy concern? (You may need to flip back to Isaiah 1:1.)

Attempt to draw a picture of the seraphim below.

The temple became the throne room of God in Isaiah's vision. He saw the seraphim, created angelic creatures whose name means "burning ones," praising God's holiness and declaring that His glory fills the earth.[20] They covered their eyes to shield them from God's magnificent glory and covered their feet as a symbol of their submission to God. Their three-fold declaration was significant. The Hebrew language uses repetition to describe something of the highest quality. To repeat something three times takes it to an even higher level. Scholar Gary V. Smith says: "Thus the seraphs claim that God is completely, totally, absolutely, the holiest of the holy. Holiness is the essence of God's nature and God himself is the supreme revelation of holiness. God's absolute holiness reveals how separate, different, or totally other he is in comparison to all other aspects of the created world."[21]

The seraphim praised the holiness of God and declared that the whole earth was filled with His glory. God's glory and holiness are inextricably linked. John Piper described it this way: "The glory of God is the manifest beauty of His holiness."[22] This vision served to commission Isaiah as a prophet. Through it he experienced the grandness, grace, and calling of the Holy One.

Read Revelation 4:1-11. Who saw this vision? Where was he at the time? (You may need to flip to earlier chapters in Revelation.) Whom did this vision concern?

Attempt to draw the creatures mentioned in this passage.

How are the visions in the Books of Isaiah and Revelation similar? How are they different?

Write out the creatures' unceasing proclamation in verse 8.

What attributes of God are displayed in this passage?

What a glorious scene as the heavenly beings declare, "Holy, holy, holy" (v. 8). God is displayed as powerful and awe-inspiring, with lightning and rolling thunder proceeding from His throne. Even the elders, who are exalted in this vision, point to the worthiness of God to be worshiped. They also act as a reminder of God's promise that those who love Him and obey His Son will one day reign with Him.

It may have felt silly to draw the creatures that praised God, but I hope it slowed your pace and gave you a moment to focus on His worthiness to be worshiped by us and every creature on the earth and in the spiritual realm. We worship the same God who was worshiped in Isaiah and Revelation. He is unchanging from eternity past to eternity future.

> Have you ever struggled with how God is presented in the Old Testament versus the New Testament? Explain. How might God seem different in each testament?

Many view the God of the Old Testament as wrathful and harsh, exemplified in His commands to Israel to wipe out pagan nations, and see the God of the New Testament as gracious and kind, sending Jesus to rescue His people from the sure consequences of sin. Yet our God is One. He is consistent throughout the Scripture.

We worship the same God who was worshiped in Isaiah and Revelation. He is unchanging from eternity past to eternity future.

He is the same yesterday, today, and forever. We see God's holy wrath for sin in the Old Testament as He punished the evil nations and in the New Testament as that wrath toward unrighteousness was laid upon Jesus and satisfied (Rom. 3:21-26). God does not respond like people but is completely holy and pure in action and motive. He never acts outside or contrary to His character.

> All God's ways are right. How does that truth comfort you? How have you seen Him work and care for you?

God is sovereign over all; nothing is outside of His direction. Moment by moment He gives us our next breath, instructs the sun to continue to shine, and cares for creatures humanity hasn't even discovered yet. He is directing all of creation toward an end that He has designed, and in His kind providence this end is for our good. He is meticulous in His care. Nothing catches Him by surprise.

He is in a class of His own, worthy of all worship. He is infinitely holy, right, and good. This is our comfort! God is not like humanity, broken by sin. He is perfectly good and right and working on our behalf. His thoughts are not our thoughts and His ways not our ways (Isa. 55:9). He can be trusted. He is near. He is good. And He is holy.

> Spend some time praying through your response to our holy God. Worship Him for being superior in all ways to any created thing and perfect in His nature and work.

And here's something else to ponder as we close.

> Read Leviticus 11:44-45 and 1 Peter 1:15-16. What instruction is given in these passages? Is this possible? Explain.

We who are children of this holy God are to model His character. That only happens as we follow Him intimately and allow Him to reflect His character through us.

> **BUILDING YOUR THEOLOGY:** Summarize today's key truth in 1–2 sentences.

> **LIVING YOUR THEOLOGY:** How does this truth affect the way you live your everyday life?

> **PRAY:** Ask God to remind you of His holiness and His perfection in all He does. Ask God to hide this truth in your heart today so that when you face difficulty, you will remember His perfection in all things.

> **MEDITATE AND MEMORIZE:** 1 Peter 1:15-16

DAY 3

GOD IS CREATOR

A beginning. We all had one. I entered this world kicking and screaming a week before Christmas a few decades ago, and one day I'll leave it (ideally not kicking and screaming and many decades from now). Every earthly thing has a beginning and an end. But there was never a time when God was not God. There was no time before Him. He is the beginning and was present when time as we know it began. He is the Creator and Source of all things.

> Read Psalm 90:1-4. What does this passage say about God's eternal and infinite nature?

God has always been and will always be. He is the uncreated Creator, infinite in His existence and His attributes. He is infinitely good, infinitely holy, and infinitely faithful. He is all-powerful and all-knowing. He is infinitely transcendent—distinct from and superior to humanity. And in His infinite love, God chose to create.

> Read Genesis 1. How was each person of the Trinity active in creation? (See Gen. 1:1-2; John 1:3.)

The word for "beginning" in Genesis 1:1 is *re'shiyth*, which is often paired with its Hebrew antonym *a'harit*, the word for "end." The author could have and would have chosen a different word if this association wasn't intended.[23] It seems that even in the beginning, God had the glorious end in mind. God is indeed a good and kind Creator.

> Read Genesis 1:3-5. How did God create?

What does the way in which God created tell us
about Him?

The Artist had no tools and no materials. He created out of nothing
(Heb. 11:3). Simply by speaking He tilted the earth just right on its
axis so that we'd be warm enough to live but not burned to a crisp.
He spoke and animals had muscles to move and blood coursing
through their veins. He created in a moment the functions, patterns,
and scientific laws (you know, the ones I couldn't remember on my
physics final back in the day).

Read Genesis 1:6-25. What repeated phrase describes
God's evaluation of His creation?

All of God's work was good because He is infinitely good. Before
resting, God did His best work: He created man and woman in
His image. Throughout the creative process, even as the powerful
Creator, He showed Himself to be a loving Father. He is all-powerful,
ruling, reigning, filling the earth with His creation, and subduing it in
His great sovereignty.

Read Psalm 19:1-2. What does this verse tell us about
creation?

Creation proclaims the one true God. The consistency of the rising
and setting of the sun, and the moon and stars in their courses,
reveal God. Creation proclaims the power of God who makes all
things new and is faithful in all things. Yet no one would know
Jesus simply by taking note of the sun's patterns. What's evident in
creation is what we call _general revelation_, being able to see God's
fingerprints all over everything.[24]

Special revelation is the supernatural revelation of God through Scripture and Jesus that can lead us to salvation. We enjoy the majesty of the mountains, the beauty of the ocean, and the goodness of sunshine, but it is in God's Word and the life of Jesus that we find the truth of the gospel.[25]

Did God step back after creation and let the world run on its own? Why or why not?

God doesn't need us but wants to have fellowship with us and welcomes us as His own.

God is not a watchmaker, creating the world and then leaving it to its own devices, gears moving and hands ticking without any engagement with the Maker. He draws near to His creation. Throughout Scripture we see God continually involved and working on behalf of His people. And He continues to do so today.

Why do you think God chose to create?

Read Acts 17:24-25. What does God need? What can we do for Him?

God didn't create because He was lacking. He wasn't lonely or bored, needing something to do. He is infinitely satisfied within the fellowship of the Trinity. If God created the world to meet a personal need, then He would be reliant on us for His satisfaction. But God is not served by human hands or in need of our support. He is set apart, self-sufficient, and completely content in Himself. This is good news for us as we are united in Him. He doesn't need us but wants to have fellowship with us and welcomes us as His own.

Read Isaiah 43:6b-7; Acts 17:26-28; and Revelation 4:11. What do these passages say about why God created?

God created out of love and for the purpose of His glory. We are created for the express purpose of worshiping, loving, and delighting in our Creator. The songs of crickets, the warmth of summer, and the turning of the leaves in the fall are all created to bring God glory. Languages, cultures, laughter, summer days, and even difficult, gray, gloomy days are created for His glory alone.

In what ways does God receive glory from your life? How might He receive more?

Why does it matter that God created all things for His glory? What bearing does that have on your life as you wait in a carpool line, do laundry, or go to dinner with friends?

BUILDING YOUR THEOLOGY: Summarize today's key truth in 1–2 sentences.

LIVING YOUR THEOLOGY: How does this truth affect the way you live your everyday life?

PRAY: Praise God for being the Creator of all things. Ask God to help you see His goodness and His glory in all He has created.

MEDITATE AND MEMORIZE: Revelation 4:11

DAY 4

GOD IS OUR PROMISE KEEPER

Look up the definition of the word *covenant* in a dictionary or online and write it below.

What comes to mind when you think about covenants?

When I hear the word **_covenant_**, I'm immediately taken back to my wedding day. Right after I almost tripped walking up the stairs in my high heels with two hundred pairs of wide eyes watching, the pastor issued a warning: "The marriage covenant is not to be entered into lightly." Although I was still recovering from my near-death-by-tripping-if-not-by-embarrassment, I tried to shoulder the weight of this "until death do us part" commitment.

Covenants are not like nonchalant pinky promises made between preteens whose loyalty changes with the wind. Covenants are binding agreements meant to be tenaciously honored. Fortunately, and thankfully, God is excellent at keeping His covenants. He is infinitely faithful to His promises even when His people are far from Him.

Throughout history God has been a covenant Maker with His people. Let's take a walk through the covenants made between God and humanity to give us a good picture of the story line of Scripture.

Read the following passages and summarize the promise God made to His people. Leave the "Fulfillment" column blank until prompted to fill it in later in today's study.

COVENANT	KEY TEXT	PROMISE	FULFILLMENT
Adamic covenant	Genesis 3:14-19		
Noahic covenant	Genesis 9:8-11		
Abrahamic covenant	Genesis15; 17:1-14		
Mosaic covenant	Exodus 19:3-6		
Priestly covenant	Numbers 25:12-13		
Davidic covenant	2 Samuel 7:12-16		
New Covenant	Jeremiah 31:31-34		

The template for most Old Testament covenants was similar to the Suzerain treaties employed often in the ancient Middle East. These covenants "were granted by independent and powerful overlords to dependent and weaker vassals, guaranteeing them certain benefits including protection. In return, the vassal was obligated to keep specific stipulations certifying loyalty to the suzerain alone."[26] In every Old Testament covenant between God and His people, He entered into a commitment with a much weaker party, holding to His end of the deal even when Israel failed.

Often, these ancient treaties were ratified by blood, depicted in the ceremony we find in Genesis 15. Animals were cut in two and the people making the covenant walked between, essentially saying, "If I don't hold up this covenant, may this happen to me and all those in my household." Quite the promise, right? God always kept His end of the deal even when His people were entirely unfaithful to the requirements He set forth. God is the initiator, sustainer, and fulfiller of all His promises.

Why did God establish covenants with His people?

God used covenants to draw near to His people. After Adam's fall in the garden, God continually moved the redemption story forward through covenants, eventually culminating in the new covenant made possible through the coming of Jesus. This was also a covenant sealed with blood. The writer of Hebrews said that Jesus "entered the most holy place once for all time, not by the blood of goats and calves, but by his own blood, having obtained eternal redemption" (9:12). And now "he is the mediator of a new cove- nant, so that those who are called might receive the promise of the eternal inheritance" (9:15).

Jesus is the ultimate fulfillment of every covenant.

Read 2 Corinthians 1:20. Write the first sentence of this verse below.

Jesus is the ultimate fulfillment of every covenant. Through Him, every promise God has made has been satisfied.

Revisit your list of covenants from earlier. Write beside each covenant how it was fulfilled or will be fulfilled through the story line of Scripture.

Those of us who know Christ live under the new covenant. Through Jesus' sacrifice we are made right with God. We are no longer under the condemnation of the Law because we are hidden in Jesus, who kept the Law perfectly. Instead of trying to stay within the lines of the Law, as the Israelites were tasked with doing according to the Mosaic Covenant, Jesus became the new law upon our hearts through the presence of the Holy Spirit.

God no longer reveals Himself to His people only in designated locations with countless instructions on how to approach Him. God the Father is near and able to be known because Jesus has made a way (Heb. 4:14-16). He now lives within us through the presence of the Holy Spirit, revealing God's instructions to us and giving us the power to live them out. We have communion with Him not because we have any right to do so, but because He is a promise-keeping, faithful God.

What is our right response to God's faithfulness?

When chaos ensues or sadness comes, we can rest in God's faithfulness. He has not left us, and He will comfort and guide us. His promise to deliver you from evil in the end will be accomplished, and no matter what you face on earth, there is eternal peace awaiting you in His presence.

BUILDING YOUR THEOLOGY: Summarize today's key truth in 1–2 sentences.

LIVING YOUR THEOLOGY: How does this truth affect the way you live your everyday life?

PRAY: Thank God for pursuing you even when your heart was far from Him and for sending Jesus as the fulfillment of all His covenants.

MEDITATE AND MEMORIZE: 1 Thessalonians 5:24

GOD IS A GOOD FATHER

If you ran away from home and squandered a third of your family's money, would they throw a huge party for you when you finally came back, completely broke?

Perhaps you recognize this story line from the parable of the prodigal son, also known as the parable of the good father. A parable is a story that teaches a moral or spiritual lesson. Jesus used them as a primary tool to explain God and His kingdom to the multitudes, to the disciples, and to the self-righteous Pharisees, who were the religious leaders of this day.

> Read Luke 15:1-2. What complaint did the Pharisees have against Jesus?

> Jesus responded to their complaint in Luke 15 with three different parables. List the titles of the parables below.

In these parables, Jesus revealed a God who loves the sinner and pursues the unfaithful so that they may turn to Him. This wasn't the salvation-through-works faith the Pharisees taught. How dare God be so reckless in His love that He would give it to those who have no merit! The love described in these parables isn't the love of a disconnected god who demands robotic obedience or else. This is the love of a gracious Father. The kingdom of God that Jesus came to bring allows us to experience God as our Father.

> Read Luke 15:11-32. Describe each of the two sons. What was each brother's issue, or better said, sin?

How would you describe the father's character?

Which brother do you best relate to in the story? Why?

Ancient Middle Eastern culture sheds light on this passage. Sons were the glory of their fathers, joining in the family work and living among their fathers throughout their lives. If a son left, the family could struggle to support itself, even more so if he demanded his inheritance as the younger son in this story did. The son was essentially declaring his father dead to him with his request. Land and possessions had to be sold to convert this inheritance prematurely to cash. Such a request would have caused much shame and grief for the father.

Customarily, if a wayward son returned, the village leaders would intercept him before he entered the village and perform a ceremony known as the *kezazah*. They would break a large pot in front of him and pronounce him cut off from his people, leaving him no place in the village. This ceremony would have happened long before he reached his family.[27]

But in Jesus' story, the father saw his son in the distance and sprinted to him. To run meant the father had to hitch up his robe, exposing his bare legs, which would have been considered shameful. He reached his son before the village leaders, and instead of turning his son away, he welcomed him home. We see in this parable the grace and lovingkindness of a father who doesn't shame his child but instead takes on shame for him.

How has our loving Father taken on our shame?

When the older son chose to stand outside the party and complain, the father set aside his dignity in an attempt to bring reconciliation.

Jesus challenged the Pharisees to see that the outcasts were brothers coming to life. Instead, the religious leaders were angry that the unholy were accepted so freely. Jesus also pointed them to the lavishness of God's grace and His right to show compassion to whomever He chooses. The Father's appeal to the older son represented Jesus' appeal to His opponents, inviting them to the party. Whether they decided to join or not, grace was available for all. It still is. The Father lavishly forgives those who were once far away and generously reinstates them as sons and daughters. Our God is the perfect Father.

Who are the outcasts in our society? Is your view of them the same as the Father's? Explain.

The Father lavishly forgives those who were once far away and generously reinstates them as sons and daughters.

God's perfection and goodness as Father isn't just an attribute. It is foundational to who He is. Scholar Michael Reeves says that God is Father before He is Creator or Ruler. "It is only when we see that God rules his creation as a kind and loving Father that we will be moved to delight in his providence. We might acknowledge that the rule of some heavenly policeman was just, but we could never take delight in his regime as we can delight in the tender care of a father."[28]

Those who do not yet know God may believe that He is a wrathful dictator, demanding His way. But we see the truth about His character in this parable. He is a kind, loving Father who wants good for us. Even His laws are for our good. As our Father, God is inherently providing for His children, sustaining us throughout the days of our lives. He also provides for all of creation that which it needs to continue and flourish. He is a good God.

Have you ever found it difficult to view God as your perfect, good Father? Why or why not?

I don't know what type of earthly father you have or had. Maybe your earthly father was wonderful, or maybe he was absent, abusive, or unsupportive. Or maybe you, like me, lost your dad at an early age and ache because of his death. But know this: if you trust Jesus, you are a child of God. He is your loving heavenly Father. He will not fail you and cannot lie. He is without fault, and His love for you is so extravagant that it may seem undignified, excessive, and lavish. He is always present, always listening, always providing.

How does this truth affect the way you view God? How you pray? How you live?

BUILDING YOUR THEOLOGY: Summarize today's key truth in 1–2 sentences.

LIVING YOUR THEOLOGY: How does this truth affect the way you live your everyday life?

PRAY: Thank God for being your good Father who takes on your shame so that you can be honored. Thank Him for sending His Son to die on the cross so you can be His child.

MEDITATE AND MEMORIZE: James 1:17

FURTHER STUDY: What other questions do you have about God?

RESOURCES

THE TRINITY: MISUNDERSTANDINGS

WHAT WE AFFIRM ABOUT THE TRINITY:
1. God is three Persons. They are distinct.
2. Each Person is fully God.
3. There is one God (Isa. 45:5; 1 Tim. 2:5; Jas. 2:19).[29]

WHERE TRINITY ANALOGIES FAIL:
1. The clover or shamrock:

Description: Just as one clover has three leaves, God is one God but three Persons.

Problem: In a clover, each leaf is only part of the whole. No one would say one leaf is the whole clover. This analogy denies the unity of God, and divides Him into three separate Persons. This view leads to tritheism (see next page).

2. The parts of an egg (or avocado for my hipster friends):

Description: A chicken's egg consists of a shell, egg white, and yolk.

Problem: God is not three parts of a whole. Each Person is fully God, not a three-way division of God. You could also throw away a piece of the egg and still have breakfast.

3. Forms of matter:

Description: Water exists in three forms: ice, water, and steam.

Problem: Water is one element acting in three different ways in response to conditions around it. God isn't one Person switching between functions, but three Persons.

4. Relational example:

Description: One person might be a mom, an aunt, and a sister.

Problem: This is one person fulfilling three roles (modalism, see next page).

SOME COMMON HERESIES:

Modalism: God is one Person in three forms (or modes). In this _heresy_, God acts as the Father, the Son, or the Spirit in function, but is only one in Person. Christians reject this understanding as unbiblical and affirm that God is three Persons in one essence.[30]

Tritheism: This heresy denies that there is only one God, and instead sees each Person of the Trinity as a separate God.[31]

OTHER TRINITARIAN CONTROVERSIES:

Arian Controversy: This was a series of disputes between Arius and Athanasius. Arius believed that God the Father created God the Son, so the Son is not equal to or of the same substance as the Father. Athanasius argued that God the Son is the same substance as the Father, so He must be equal. These disputes divided the church for more than fifty years, from AD 325-381 (from the Council of Nicaea to the Council of Constantinople).[32]

Subordination: This view held that Jesus was fully divine, but was not equal to the Father. This was a hot topic around the time of the Arian Controversy, but even today some hold the subordination view regarding the Son or the Spirit.[33]

There is no perfect analogy or illustration for the Trinity, and there is no shortage of heresies in the history of the church. We need to stand on these statements: God is three Persons. They are distinct. Each Person is fully God. There is one God.

FAQS

How does God reveal Himself?

We mentioned earlier in the study two ways God reveals Himself: general revelation and special revelation. General revelation consists of ways God reveals Himself through nature or natural means. Special revelation comes through supernatural means, primarily through God's Word (the Bible and the life of Jesus). God also may reveal His character, ways, and will by the Holy Spirit through the counsel of wise people, our consciences, or our circumstances.

If God knew Satan would rebel, why did He create him?

God created all things, and all He created was good. At some point between creation and Genesis 3, Satan rebelled. Because God is sovereign and all-knowing, He knew that this would occur. But just knowing about it does not mean God caused it. However, because God foreknew Satan's fall, we understand that his fall was part of God's ultimate plan to bring salvation to the world.

Can God create a rock so heavy He can't lift it?

This circular, nonsensical question is often asked by those skeptical of the Christian faith. The short answer here is no. This rock would have to be infinitely large, but rocks are material, so it could not be infinitely large. God cannot create a contradiction, which is what this question is requesting God to do.

Can God sin?

God cannot sin because that would be outside the realm of His unchanging character. This does not make God lesser because He is incapable of doing something. Instead, it makes Him transcendent and holy, separate from humanity and completely unstained by sin (Titus 1:2; Jas. 1:13).

GROUP TIME

OPEN

Begin your group time with the large group discussing the following questions:

What was the highlight of your week of study?

What was something new you learned this week?

How did this week's study challenge what you believe about God?

REVIEW AND DISCUSS

Break into smaller groups to complete this section. Use the following Scripture passages and questions to review what you learned in your personal Bible study on God.

Read Ephesians 1:3-14.
How do you see the work of each Person of the Trinity in this passage?

How would you explain the Trinity to a new Christian? Why is it so important that we get this doctrine right?

Read Isaiah 6:1-4.
What does it mean for God to be holy?

How do we often diminish this attribute of God? What's the danger in doing so?

Read Genesis 1:1-5.
What does the way God created tell us about Him?

How does all of creation, including us, give glory to God?

Read 2 Corinthians 1:19-20.
How is Jesus the fulfillment of every promise of God?

How have you seen God keep His promises to you?

Read Luke 15:20-24.
How does the parable of the prodigal son in Luke 15 show us the goodness of God?

How have you experienced the goodness of God even in difficult times?

REFLECT AND APPLY
Spend a moment writing your answers to the following questions, then discuss with your small group.

What other questions about God did this week's study raise?

What's your main takeaway from this study on God?

Why does what you believe about God matter?

What will you do this week to know God more intimately?

CLOSE
Close with worship, taking turns in your group naming different attributes of God, and thanking and praising Him for who He is.

JESUS

SESSION 3

JESUS IS FULLY GOD AND FULLY MAN

Well, here we are, throwing caution to the wind and plunging headlong into Christology like a kid diving straight into the deep end of the pool on the first day of summer. So take your phone out of your pocket, put that towel on the chair, and jump in!

List some key truths about God the Son.

God the Son has been with the Father and Holy Spirit since before time began. All things were created through Him (John 1:3), and He possesses all the attributes shared within the Trinity. He was sent by God the Father to become flesh, conceived by the Spirit in Mary's womb, born in an animal's stall, and named Jesus. When God the Son became man (called the _incarnation_), He took on human nature, making Him fully, one hundred percent man. Yet in becoming fully man, Jesus did not give up His divinity, so He remained fully, one hundred percent God.

Jesus is not two persons—one divine and one human—in one body. He is not one person operating in two personalities. He is fully God and fully man, two natures perfectly united together (called the _hypostatic union_). As God the Son in flesh, He is perfectly one with God the Father and God the Holy Spirit, as seen in John 10:30 when Jesus said, "I and the Father are one."

Read Philippians 2:1-11. What Christlike attitude or mind-set did Paul instruct the church at Philippi to adopt?

Paul quickly jumped into practical instruction early in his letter to the Philippians, then masterfully revealed key truths about Jesus, showing the "why" behind his instruction. Paul said the church was to have the same humble attitude that led Jesus from heaven to earth.

Verses 6-11 are thought to have been a hymn sung by the early church to remind them of Jesus' human and divine nature. These verses also portrayed the humility it took for Jesus to submit Himself to the ailments of having a human nature. He entered the world as a needy baby, grew through the awkward preteen stage, died a painful death as a man, and then was exalted in His resurrection and ascension. Jesus' obedience to God's plan is an example of ultimate humility.

> Read Philippians 2:6-7 again. What key characteristics of God the Son are mentioned here?

This word "existing" in verse 6 refers to God the Son's eternal nature. He has been and will always be. The "form" of God is the Greek word *morphe*, which "refers to that form which truly and fully expresses the being which underlies it."[34] God the Son, who became flesh as Jesus, is "the permanent unchangeable pattern of deity."[35]

> What does it mean that Jesus "did not consider equality with God as something to be exploited" or grasped (v. 6)?

Jesus didn't need to work hard to gain equality with God or scrape and scramble to keep it. He already had it and was secure in it. But He didn't exploit His secure position for His own gain. He didn't seek to exalt Himself. Instead, He humbly served.

> What do you think Jesus "emptied" Himself of (v. 7)?

Jesus did not surrender His deity but placed Himself in submission to the Father. He gave up His glory for a time to experience the pain and brokenness of our world and the needs that come with having a physical body. This emptying did not make Him any less God.

How do verses 9-11 reinforce that Jesus is God?

Jesus was obedient to the point of death, resurrected three days later, then ascended to the right hand of the Father (Col. 3:1). He is the exalted Savior and worthy of our worship. And one day, all people will bow before Him!

JESUS' DEITY

Why does it matter if Jesus is fully God? How do the following passages answer this question?

Colossians 1:15-20

Hebrews 9:11-15

Hebrews 10:11-15

If Jesus wasn't God, then we can't actually be saved. He would just be a good man who died a needless death.

Only God could bear the penalty for sin. Only God could be a spotless sacrifice to cover sin, and only Someone who is fully God could be the Mediator between God and man (1 Tim. 2:5). If Jesus wasn't God, then we can't actually be saved. He would just be a good man who died a needless death.

JESUS' HUMANITY

Why does it matter if Jesus is fully man? How do the following passages help answer this question?

Romans 5:12-19

1 Corinthians 15:20-22

Only Jesus could be the sinless substitute for us, dying the death we deserved and giving us His righteousness in exchange.

Sin came into the world through one man, Adam. From Adam we all inherit a sinful nature. Since sin entered through a man, it had to be removed by a man. But no sinful man could be the sacrifice. Only Jesus could be the sinless substitute for us, dying the death we deserved and giving us His righteousness in exchange.

Is Jesus just a good man, a good teacher? No! If that's all He is then we're still lost in our sin, hopelessly condemned. Rather, He is fully divine and fully human, as the Scripture testifies. He has rescued us, redeemed us, and atoned for our sin. He is the Messiah! He is the Christ! He has made a way for us to be right with God, to be part of His eternal family. And nothing will ever "separate us from the love of God that is in Christ Jesus our Lord" (Rom. 8:39). Hallelujah!

Read John 1:1-18. Today's session has been heavy, but I hope this beautiful passage is a benediction for you.

BUILDING YOUR THEOLOGY: Summarize today's key truth in 1–2 sentences.

LIVING YOUR THEOLOGY: How does this truth affect the way you live your everyday life?

PRAY: Thank Jesus for humbling Himself and coming to earth to be your Savior. Thank Him for being your sinless sacrifice to redeem you and give you eternal life.

MEDITATE AND MEMORIZE: Colossians 1:15

JESUS IS THE PROMISED MESSIAH

Describe a time when you had a difficult period of waiting.

Waiting can be agonizing. Just the word *tryouts* makes me shudder when I think about having to wait for the posted results. And I'm certain the earth spins more slowly on its axis the days between having a "this looks weird" spot removed from my skin and the phone call with the results. I struggle to focus on anything but the resolution I desperately want.

The people of Israel waited for generations for God to fulfill His promise to send a Deliverer. They longed to be out from under the weight of their oppression. They celebrated the promise of His coming with annual festivals, and they memorized prophecies about His coming. Yet when He arrived, few recognized Him.

The Bible story of Simeon is one of my favorites. He was no stranger to waiting, to faithfully holding to God's promise of a coming Deliverer. Finally, as an old man, Simeon was one of the first to identify Jesus as the Messiah.

Read Luke 2:25-35.

God the Son had come, ushering in the new covenant. Simeon's words were filled with both prophecy and fulfillment.

What was fulfilled (vv. 29-32)?

What was prophesied to Mary (vv. 34-35)?

The Messiah had come, bringing salvation for all people—Gentiles and Jews. But the message was tinged with sadness. This salvation would be costly.

How would Simeon's prophecy to Mary be fulfilled?

Simeon's words about the Messiah echoed what had been foretold throughout the Old Testament.

Read the verses below and summarize each prophecy.
• **Genesis 3:15**

• **Micah 5:2**

• **Isaiah 7:14**

• **Isaiah 9:6-7**

• **Isaiah 53:1-6**

• **Isaiah 61:1-2**

Jesus fulfilled (or will fulfill) every prophecy written about Him in Scripture, which most scholars agree is more than three hundred.[36]

If Jesus fulfilled (or will fulfill) every prophecy written about Him, what does that tell us about Scripture?

Jesus' fulfillment of every prophecy further confirms the inspiration of Scripture. If Scripture wasn't without error and God-breathed, surely the human authors would have gotten one wrong, right?

The probability of one person fulfilling just eight of the prophecies is astounding. It would be like placing 100,000,000,000,000,000 silver dollars on the ground throughout all of Texas, marking one of these coins with an X, and expecting a blindfolded friend to pick up the marked coin. The likelihood of them finding it is 1 in 10^{17}. [37]

The Messiah has come, fully God and fully man, to deliver us.

Many of the circumstances surrounding these prophecies included uncontrollable details like birthplace, lineage, and type of death. No one would be able to fulfill them all even if the person were unbelievably successful at deception and marking tasks off a list.

What are other religions waiting for? Why do they not recognize Jesus as Messiah? How do they differ from Christianity?

If these questions were difficult for you to answer, get to know some people who worship differently than you and begin reading about other religions. It will strengthen your beliefs and will help you better share the good news of Jesus with those who believe differently.

Many religions see Jesus as a good teacher. They even claim to worship the God of the Bible. But they don't affirm Jesus as the Messiah or see Him as fully God. Even Jews, who worship the God of the Bible, don't believe Jesus is God. They are still looking for a coming Messiah. Yet we know the Messiah has come, fully God and fully man, to deliver us. He lived, died, rose again, and is now seated at the right hand of the Father.

How would you explain the deliverance that Jesus offers?

Jesus, the exalted Messiah, came to offer deliverance, but it wasn't from the power of other nations. He brought spiritual freedom, liberating us through His life, death, and resurrection. We live free of the eternal consequences and chains of sin and death. We are free to enjoy God and His presence forever. Hallelujah!

Jesus, the exalted Messiah, came to offer deliverance, but it wasn't from the power of other nations. He brought spiritual freedom.

How would our lives be different if we were still waiting on the Messiah to come?

If the Messiah hasn't actually come, then we are in trouble. We are still under the Law, unable to reach God. We still stand condemned for our sins, facing the wrath of God. But because of Jesus, the atoning sacrifice, we have been made right with God. The Messiah has come to redeem us.

If Jesus was just a good teacher, then we should read His words like any other book. But since He is the Messiah, we should fall at His feet in worship, devour and obey His Word, and share the good news of the gospel.

BUILDING YOUR THEOLOGY: Summarize today's key truth in 1–2 sentences.

LIVING YOUR THEOLOGY: How does this truth affect the way you live your everyday life?

PRAY: Thank God for providing proof to help us trust that Jesus really is the Savior sent to redeem all who trust Him. Thank God for sending prophets and for inspiring humans to write His Word so that we could know Him.

MEDITATE AND MEMORIZE: Isaiah 9:6-7

JESUS IS GOD WITH US

Have you ever felt like God didn't care about or understand what you were going through? When?

From the beginning, God wanted to be near His people. In Genesis 1:2, the Spirit of God hovered over the waters, near to the earth that would soon host so much life.

It seems there was intimate fellowship between God and man in the garden of Eden. Genesis 3:8 describes how Adam and Eve, just after having listened to the serpent and disobeying God by eating the fruit, heard God walking in the garden. I know it's speculation, but God's action doesn't seem out of the norm for Adam and Eve. I imagine God communed with them often.

During Israel's exodus from Egypt, God led His people with a cloud by day and a pillar of fire by night; He met with Moses on Mount Sinai; and He provided food and water in the wilderness. He moved even closer to His people with the construction of the tabernacle, then the temple. God was ever moving closer. Then, in the ultimate act of nearness, God sent Jesus, Immanuel, "God with us."

Read Luke 2:1-20.

God became flesh. He was conceived by the Holy Spirit, resulting in a virgin birth. His entrance into the world occurred in one of the most unsophisticated of places. Our Lord and Savior was laid where animals fed, completely dependent on Mary and Joseph.

Take a minute to ask as many questions as you can about the Luke 2 passage.

The baby Jesus grew into a wobbly-legged toddler, a kid who skinned His knees, and maybe even a teen dealing with acne. Scripture doesn't tell us much about His growing-up years. We do know He gave His parents a scare at age twelve when He, unbeknownst to them, stayed behind in Jerusalem while they headed back to Nazareth after Passover (Luke 2:41-50). And evidently He learned carpentry from Joseph (Mark 6:3). It seems Jesus lived the normal life of His day, similar to what you and I do today.

Jesus launched into ministry around age thirty. Keep in mind that Jesus' name means *God saves*, while Christ means *Messiah* or *Anointed One*. Christ isn't Jesus' last name but a declaration of who He is. He was anointed by God for a specific task, and His ministry would proclaim this.

"The Word became flesh and blood, and moved into the neighborhood."

JOHN 1:14
THE MESSAGE

Read Mark 1:9-11. What is significant about the baptism of Jesus?

His baptism wasn't a baptism of repentance, because Jesus was sinless. Instead, it could have been an act of obedience to the Father, a way to identify with sinful humanity, or an affirmation of John the Baptist's ministry. What is certain is the confirmation Jesus received as God the Father expressed His approval and the Spirit descended on Jesus, indicating anointing and empowerment for ministry. All who were gathered on the shore that day could trust that what Jesus said was true. Jesus' baptism marked the beginning of His public ministry.

Through Jesus' ministry, we see clearly how God is with us. Jesus could have come into the world and been aloof, standoffish. He could have directed things from an isolated palace. But instead, He came to be with us, to be near us. As Eugene Peterson paraphrased,

"The Word became flesh and blood,
and moved into the neighborhood."
JOHN 1:14, THE MESSAGE

Peruse the following passages and note some of the things Jesus did and experienced:

Matthew 4:1-11

Mark 2:13-17

Mark 3:20-21

John 2:1-2

John 4:4-8

He was tempted. He spent time with friends. He had a family that didn't understand. He went to weddings. He got tired and thirsty. He was a common person among common people doing common things. He came near, understanding everyday life because He lived it. Even His teachings weren't lofty theological treatises, but simple stories from everyday life with profound meanings.

Read the following passages and note the common life context and messages of each teaching.

SCRIPTURE	CONTEXT	MESSAGE
Matthew 5:13-16		
Luke 6:43		
Luke 13:18-19		

Being with us prepared Him to minister for us and to us.

Read Hebrews 2:17-18. For what two reasons did Jesus come to be with us?

The God of the universe is for us and understands because He has been here.

He had to be like us to be the sacrifice for us. The high priest interceded for the people, offering sacrifices for their sin. But Jesus is the Great High Priest, offering Himself as our atoning sacrifice to free us from sin eternally.

And He also was like us so that He could help us. We are not on an island. The God of the universe is for us and understands us because He has been here. Jesus lived this life and suffered temptation and pain. But He doesn't just know our pain; He has the power to help us in our pain.

The King of heaven left His throne to walk the dust of the earth in order to rescue and restore those made from the dust of the earth.

BUILDING YOUR THEOLOGY: Summarize today's key truth in 1–2 sentences.

LIVING YOUR THEOLOGY: How does this truth affect the way you live your everyday life?

PRAY: Thank God for coming near in Christ to be with us, to be like us, to love us, and to rescue us. Spend some time thanking Him for the specific ways He has met your needs in trying times and difficult situations.

MEDITATE AND MEMORIZE: Mark 1:15

JESUS IS SAVIOR AND LORD

Jesus shedding His blood as an atoning sacrifice was not a surprise. It was foreshadowed in the Old Testament through blood spilled during circumcision—the sign of the Abrahamic covenant—the blood of the Passover lamb on the doorposts of Israelite families in Egypt, and the sacrificial system administered by the priests.

When God gave Moses the Law, He expected His people to obey. Obedience was the right response to God's provision, but Israel wasn't very good at obedience. (I don't know about you, but I see a lot of myself in the Israelites.) So God made a way for them to be made right with Him. He created a sacrificial system in the tabernacle (and later the temple) to make appropriate *atonement* for their sin. The most important sacrifice took place on the Day of Atonement.

> Read Leviticus 16:3-10,15-22. List the things the high priest was to do on the Day of Atonement.

> What was the significance of the two goats?

The Day of Atonement happened once a year in the temple. On this day, the priest traded his beautiful garments for white linen as a symbol of repentance. He offered a sin offering for himself and his family, sprinkling the blood of the sacrifice within the holy of holies, on the mercy seat of the ark of the covenant.

Then one goat was sacrificed and its blood was sprinkled on the altar. This was a life-for-life example of the grave nature of sin. Through this sacrifice, the required punishment for sin was satisfied and forgiveness secured.

The priest then confessed the sins of the nation while laying his hands on the other goat's head, and that goat was sent away. He was the scapegoat, taking the sin of the people far from them.

These sacrifices were never meant to be a final atonement for sin. They were temporary and insufficient (Heb. 10:1,4). Jesus was the life-for-life exchange for us. He substituted Himself for us and paid our penalty (*penal substitution*) once for all (Heb. 10:10).

> Read Mark 15–16. What strikes you most from this account of Jesus' crucifixion and resurrection?

Jesus' death took place on the day of Passover, which by Jesus' time was considered the first day of the Feast of Unleavened Bread (Mark 14:12; 15:42).

> What is the significance of Jesus being crucified on Passover?

Passover commemorated Israel's deliverance from slavery in Egypt (Ex. 12). The tenth plague on Egypt was the death of every firstborn male. But God protected the Israelites, instructing them to place the blood of a lamb on their doorposts (v. 13). He would then lead them out of their oppression.

Generations later, Jesus would be the perfect sacrificial Lamb, covering us by His blood and protecting us from the wrath of God toward sin.

> Why do you think it was necessary for Jesus to die?

Read Romans 3:10-26. How does this passage help answer the previous question?

All of us have sinned. All of us are unrighteous and separated from God. There is no way for us, in our own power or merit, to reconcile ourselves to God. So God made a way for us. God is holy and hates sin. That's not a choice He made; that's His character. And God never acts outside His character. He couldn't just ignore our sin. Sin had to be judged and punished. So God sent Jesus to be the _propitiation_, the atoning sacrifice for our sins. On the cross, Jesus took on the crushing wrath of God for sin. He was flogged, mocked, humiliated, nailed to a cross, and left to die, not because of anything He did, but because He willingly and obediently traded places with us. Paul stated it like this:

Just as the blood of a lamb saved the Israelites, the blood of the Lamb has saved us.

> "He made the one who did not know sin to be sin for us, so
> that in him we might become the righteousness of God."
> **2 CORINTHIANS 5:21**

Jesus took our place. He lived the perfect life of obedience we couldn't live and then became the perfect sacrifice for our sins. Just as the blood of a lamb saved the Israelites, the blood of the Lamb has saved us.

Read the following passages and note what the blood of Jesus does for us: Romans 3:25; 5:8-9; Ephesians 1:7; 1 Peter 1:18-19; 1 John 1:7.

Jesus is the Mediator of a new and better covenant. He is the sacrifice on our behalf. He died once and for all on the cross to pay for sin, and He rose again proving that the payment had been accepted and that sin, death, and evil were defeated forever. But what if Jesus had just stayed dead?

Read 1 Corinthians 15:12-22 and summarize why the resurrection is so important.

The resurrection has validated the power of God and has proclaimed Christ's power over sin and death.

Paul said that if the resurrection is not true, then Christ's death has no meaning. Our faith is worthless and we are still in our sins. But the resurrection *did* happen. It validated the power of God and proclaimed Christ's power over sin and death. His resurrection paves the way for ours. We will live forever with Him because Jesus has made a way.

Jesus is the risen Savior, now seated at the right hand of God. All who are hidden in Him will not pay for sin at judgment because God is just and will only punish sin once. Jesus fully absorbed God's wrath as the righteous payment for sin.

Because of what Jesus did, and because of His authority as God, we owe Him everything. We are called to trust Him as Savior and surrender to Him as Lord. It's not one or the other; it's both.

BUILDING YOUR THEOLOGY: Summarize today's key truth in 1–2 sentences.

LIVING YOUR THEOLOGY: How does this truth affect the way you live your everyday life?

PRAY: If you've yet to trust Christ as your Savior and Lord, do so now. Pray, repenting of your sins and professing your faith in Christ to save you. If you've already made that decision, spend a moment thanking Jesus for the precious gift of your salvation.

MEDITATE AND MEMORIZE: 2 Corinthians 5:21

JESUS IS PROPHET, PRIEST, AND KING

Write the first duty or phrase that comes to mind when you think of the following:

PROPHET	PRIEST	KING

Read Revelation 1:4-6.

The concept of *munus triplex*, or Jesus as Prophet, Priest, and King, is seen in three statements in verses 5-6:

- "the faithful witness" (Prophet);
- "the firstborn from the dead" (Priest);
- "the ruler of the kings of the earth" (King). [38]

Jesus fulfilling these three offices is not suddenly introduced in the final book of the Bible. Jesus as Prophet, Priest, and King is discussed in other New Testament passages and foreshadowed in the Old Testament as well.

PROPHET
In the Old Testament, prophets were God's mouthpieces, speaking truth and foretelling the future. The prophets were also known to perform miracles. Jesus performed those same functions.

Read the following passages and note how Jesus fulfilled the role of prophet in each one.

Matthew 17:22-23	
Mark 1:21-22	
Mark 1:32-34	
Luke 7:11-17	
John 13:36-38	

In the Luke 7 passage, Jesus raised a young man from the dead, and all the people began to proclaim that He was a prophet. It's doubtful they understood that He was the Prophet who had come to fulfill all prophecy. He was not a prophet sent to just speak a word from God, He was the final word, the ultimate word, the Word made flesh (John 1:1). Jesus fulfilled the role of Prophet as the ultimate teacher, the ultimate revelation of God.

How does Jesus as Prophet matter to your everyday life?

PRIEST

The priestly system established by God through the line of Aaron, Moses' brother, was a beautiful foreshadowing of what was to come. Priests were the mediators between God and man. As the mediator, the high priest would enter the holy of holies on the Day of Atonement and offer a sacrifice for the sins of the people. Hebrews 4–10 shows how Jesus is the better High Priest.

Read Hebrews 7:18-28; 9:11-15. What makes it possible for Jesus to be the final and Great High Priest?

Jesus has entered the holy of holies and offered the ultimate sacrifice for us—Himself. As our High Priest, He has made a way for us.

> Read Hebrews 4:14-16. Because of Jesus, how can we approach God's throne? What do we find when we get there?

> Take a moment to offer thanks for this open access to God, and lay before Him the difficulties you are currently facing.

KING

> What do the following passages say about the kingship of Jesus?
>
> Matthew 28:18
>
> Luke 1:30-33
>
> Hebrews 1:7-8
>
> Hebrews 12:2

Jesus has entered the holy of holies and offered the ultimate sacrifice for us—Himself. As our High Priest, He has made a way for us.

All authority and power are His. He reigns supreme. Jesus sits at God's right hand and intercedes for His people, acting as not only ruling King but interceding Priest. His crucifixion was a coronation—a crown was placed on His head, a robe around His shoulders, and a sign above Him declaring Him King. His resurrection declared sin and death defeated, lauding Him as the victorious King. As Jeremy Treat wrote in *The Crucified King*, "The cross is the apex of Jesus' kingdom mission and the kingdom is the aim of the cross."[39]

Jesus the King wants to be king of your life.

What are you tempted to place in the seat of authority in your life?

It's so easy to allow your task list or your role as wife, mom, or employee to determine how you spend your days and your life. But doing so removes God from His rightful throne and puts an idol in His place. There are dozens of things we can put on the pedestals of our hearts, but they are powerless to help us. Jesus the King is advocating for us, ruling over our hearts and all of creation.

Read Hebrews 1:1-4, and note where you see each of Jesus' three offices (Prophet, Priest, and King) represented:

Jesus is the Word of God, our Mediator who has cleansed us of sin and now reigns as King at the right hand of the Father. Hallelujah!

BUILDING YOUR THEOLOGY: Summarize today's key truth in 1–2 sentences.

LIVING YOUR THEOLOGY: How does this truth affect the way you live your everyday life?

PRAY: Thank Jesus for advocating for you as Your High Priest, for His control over your life as King, and for proclaiming and being the Word made flesh as Prophet.

MEDITATE AND MEMORIZE: Hebrews 1:2-3

FURTHER STUDY: What other questions do you have about God the Son?

RESOURCES

CHRISTOLOGY HERESIES AND COUNCILS
EARLY CHURCH HERESIES

Any departure from Jesus as fully God and fully man is considered heresy, or counter to the truth of Scripture. This includes believing:

- Jesus is only God or only man

- Jesus seemed to be human but wasn't really

- Jesus is two separate persons who simply work together

To combat these heresies (and others), the church held ecumenical councils, crafting statements of belief. Two of the most important councils were held at Nicaea and Chalcedon. The creeds they developed are provided. Many of the heresies were a misunderstanding or misinterpretation of Scripture. This is a good reminder for us to diligently study our Bibles. If not, we could believe and even advocate for something that is false.

EARLY CHURCH COUNCILS
Council of Nicaea (AD 325)

This council was convened by the Roman emperor Constantine and focused on the eternal deity of Christ. At this council the Nicene Creed was developed. Further amendments were made to the creed in AD 381 at the Council of Constantinople. Read the Nicene Creed below.

"We believe ... in one Lord Jesus Christ, the only-begotten Son of God, begotten of the Father before all the ages, Light of Light, true God of true God, begotten not made, of one substance with the Father, through whom all things were made; who for us men and for our salvation came down from the heavens, and was made flesh of the Holy Spirit and the Virgin Mary, and became man, and was crucified for us under Pontius Pilate, and suffered and was buried, and rose again on the third day according to the Scriptures, and ascended into the heavens, and sat down on the right hand of the Father, and will come again with glory to judge the living and dead, of whose kingdom there shall be no end." [40]

Council of Chalcedon (AD 451)

This council was convened by the emperor Marcian and was the fourth ecumenical council of the Christian church. This council confirmed that Jesus is one Person with two natures, both human and divine, developing the following Chalcedonian Creed:

"Following the holy fathers, we all with one accord teach men to acknowledge one and the same Son, our Lord Jesus Christ, at once complete in divinity and complete in manhood, truly God and truly man, consisting also of a rational soul and body; of one substance [homoousios] with the Father as regards his Godhead, and at the same time of one substance with us as regards his manhood; like us in all respects, apart from sin; as regards his Godhead, begotten of the Father before the ages, but yet as regards his manhood begotten [born], for us men and for our salvation, of Mary the virgin, the God-bearer [theotokos]; one and the same Christ, Son, Lord, only-begotten, recognized in two natures, without confusion, without change, without division, without separation; the distinction of natures being in no way annulled by the union, but rather the characteristics of each nature begin preserved and coming together to form one person and subsistence [hypostasis], not as parted or separated into two persons, but one and the same Son and only-begotten God the Word, Lord Jesus Christ.[41]

"Therefore, following the holy fathers, we all with one accord teach men to acknowledge one and the same Son, our Lord Jesus Christ, at once complete in Godhead and complete in manhood, truly God and truly man, consisting also of a reasonable soul and body; of one substance with the Father as regards his Godhead, and at the same time of one substance with us as regards his manhood; like us in all respects, apart from sin; as regards his Godhead, begotten of the Father before the ages, but yet as regards his manhood begotten, for us men and for our salvation, of Mary the Virgin, the God-bearer; one and the same Christ, Son, Lord, Only-begotten, recognized in two natures, without confusion, without change, without division, without separation; the distinction of natures being in no way annulled by the union, but rather the characteristics of each nature being preserved and coming together to form one person and subsistence, not as parted or separated into two persons, but one and the same Son and Only-begotten God the Word, Lord Jesus Christ; even as the prophets from earliest times spoke of him, and our Lord Jesus Christ himself taught us, and the creed of the fathers has handed down to us."[42]

FAQS

How is Jesus' resurrection different from others in Scripture who were raised from the dead?
Others who were brought back to life in Scripture, such as Lazarus, were restored to life in an earthly body and experienced death again. However Jesus was raised in His resurrected body, one that will exist eternally. He was the "firstfruits" (1 Cor. 15:20,23), meaning He was the first to be resurrected and represented more to come.

How are we united in Christ?
We are united with Jesus in His crucifixion (Gal. 2:20), burial (Col. 2:12), resurrection (Rom. 6:5), and seated with Him in heavenly places (Eph. 2:6). Christ is in us (2 Cor. 13:5) and we are in Him (1 Cor. 1:30). This is mysterious, but it is through this union that we are hidden in Christ, declared righteous, made heirs, and adopted into God's family. All the benefits of our faith are wrapped up in being united with Christ.

Why did Jesus seem to break laws (specifically the Sabbath)?
First, Jesus did not break God's Law. If He had, He would have sinned, and Scripture affirms many times that He was sinless (2 Cor. 5:21: Heb. 4:15; 1 Pet. 2:22). The actions Jesus took on the Sabbath that angered the religious leaders broke with their tradition but not the Law of God.

Why is the ascension significant?
The ascension marked the end of Jesus' earthly ministry and the return to His heavenly glory. It also began the time of His preparation of our heavenly home (John 14:2) and His work as High Priest, ever interceding for us before the Father (Rom. 8:34). And because He ascended, we can trust that He will return in the same way He went (Acts 1:9-11).

GROUP TIME

OPEN

Begin your group time with the large group discussing the following questions:

What was the highlight of your week of study?

What was something new you learned this week?

How did this week's study challenge what you believe about Jesus?

REVIEW AND DISCUSS

Break into smaller groups to complete this section. Use the following Scripture passages and questions to review what you learned in your personal Bible study on Jesus.

Read Philippians 2:5-11.
Why was it vital for Jesus to be both fully God and fully man?

How would you explain this concept of fully God, fully man to an unbeliever who is curious about Jesus?

Read Luke 2:25-32.
What kind of Messiah were the people of Israel looking for? How was Jesus different than their expectations?

How do we often shape Jesus to be the Messiah we want Him to be rather than the One we need?

Read John 1:14.
Throughout history, how has God shown His desire to be near us?

How has the nearness of Jesus been a comfort to you over the past few days?

Read 2 Corinthians 5:21.
Why did Jesus have to die?

Why is the resurrection so important?

Read Hebrews 1:1-4.
How has Jesus fulfilled the roles of Prophet, Priest, and King?

How has Jesus been Prophet, Priest, and King to you?

REFLECT AND APPLY

Spend a moment writing your answers to the following questions, then discuss with your small group.

What other questions about Jesus did this week's study raise?

What's your main takeaway from this study on Jesus?

Why does what you believe about Jesus matter?

What friend, neighbor, or family member needs to know the truth about Jesus? What will you do this week to share this truth?

CLOSE

Pray for the friends, neighbors, and family members mentioned who do not know Christ. Pray they would be drawn to Him and have hearts tender to the gospel. Pray for each other to be bold in sharing the gospel.

THE HOLY SPIRIT

SESSION 4

DAY 1

THE HOLY SPIRIT IS GOD

I don't remember talking about the Holy Spirit much growing up. This wasn't intentional; He just didn't come up in conversation or teaching as often as God the Father or God the Son. Perhaps it's because He seems more mysterious. Or perhaps there was a bit of fear that if we focused on the Spirit "things might get out of hand."

Even today it seems difficult at times to wrap our minds around the Person and work of God the Spirit. There are concrete examples of God the Father's work in creation and His presence with His people through the tabernacle or temple. And the work of God the Son incarnate recorded in the Gospels seems tangible. But an air of mystery continues to surround the Holy Spirit.

> Did you grow up talking about the Holy Spirit? Write what you know to be true about Him.

> Read Matthew 28:16-20. How did Jesus reveal His authority as God in this passage? What indicates the Holy Spirit has authority as God?

Jesus instructed His disciples to baptize in the name of all three Persons of the Trinity, naming the Holy Spirit within the Godhead. If the Holy Spirit isn't God, it would be absolutely scandalous (and heretical) for Jesus to include Him here. But the Holy Spirit is one with God the Father and God the Son.

> Why does it matter that the Holy Spirit is God?

Read John 14:15-21. How long will the Holy Spirit be with us?

The Holy Spirit is in us and with us. It's a mystery but a beautiful one!

How is the Holy Spirit described in this passage?

The Greek words in verse 16 for "another Counselor" are *allos* ("another of the same kind")[43] and *parakletos* (Comforter, Advocate).[44] This Spirit is "of the same kind" as God the Son, and He is our Paraklete, or one who comes to our aid. He aids and comforts us and provides an irreversible affirmation that we are God's. He teaches us and transforms our hearts so that our affections and responses become more and more like Jesus. The Holy Spirit is in us and with us. It's a mystery but a beautiful one!

Before Jesus ascended, He told His disciples to wait in Jerusalem for the coming of the Holy Spirit (Acts 1:4-5). They waited and He came with power.

Read Acts 2:1-12. Describe this scene in your own words.

Jerusalem was a central city for trade, so every day the city was humming with different people and languages. This was especially true during Pentecost (also called the Festival of Weeks). Pentecost was one of Israel's three annual pilgrimage feasts where Jews from various nations would come to Jerusalem to celebrate. Often, those visiting Jerusalem would either communicate with each other in a shared language or be unable to communicate for the duration of their time in Jerusalem.[45] Can you imagine the amazement and confusion as travelers heard the familiar sound of their languages spoken in a land far from home?

While Israel celebrated God's provision of the harvest at Pentecost, God was giving them an even better provision of His presence. The Holy Spirit wouldn't just live among God's people; He would live within them.

How was the power of the Holy Spirit tangibly felt and seen on Pentecost?

Why do you think some sneered at what was taking place (v. 13)?

The Holy Spirit is the abiding blessing and power for God's people forever.

How do people still sneer at the work of the Holy Spirit today?

The coming of the Holy Spirit and His power wasn't simply for those first followers of Christ gathered in Jerusalem. Those who spoke different languages in this moment would later take the gospel to the ends of the earth through the power of the Holy Spirit. And this same empowering Spirit lives today in those who trust Jesus.

The Holy Spirit is the abiding blessing and power for God's people forever. He will never leave, never change, and never tire of counseling, loving, and empowering you, both in the huge events of your life and the mundane, everyday decisions you make. He is God, possessing all power and authority. That's been true from the very beginning (Gen. 1:2) and will be true to the end. It is through His power that Jesus was raised from the dead (Rom. 8:11). This same God is living within you!

For what situations in your life do you need the Holy Spirit's comfort? Counsel? Power?

How is your life different when you're relying on the Holy Spirit?

Our God is intimately involved and aware of our everyday questions, doubts, and triumphs because He lives within us. He is well acquainted with the dark closets of our hearts that we'd rather Him not try to spring clean. Yet He gently convicts us of our sin, calling us to holy living. He guides, comforts, and empowers us. He lives in us and works in us to make us more like Jesus.

BUILDING YOUR THEOLOGY: Summarize today's key truth in 1–2 sentences.

LIVING YOUR THEOLOGY: How does this truth affect the way you live your everyday life?

PRAY: Take a moment to consider the reality, power, and authority of the Holy Spirit as part of the Godhead. Thank God for the Holy Spirit's presence in your life and for the Spirit's work in making you more like Jesus.

MEDITATE AND MEMORIZE: Matthew 28:19-20

DAY 2

THE HOLY SPIRIT IS OUR GUIDE

> Read John 14:26; 16:13. Describe how the Holy Spirit
> teaches us and guides us according to these verses.

I've often wished the Holy Spirit would speak to me in an audible voice. Or just hit some "take over all functions" button that would override the moments I open my big mouth and insert foot or do something ridiculous that I quickly regret. While He hasn't force-fully taken control to steer me in the right direction, He does use Scripture, the counsel of wise friends, and my conscience to reveal when my thoughts and actions are not in line with His truth and character. He may not audibly direct, but He does quietly guide.

> Peruse John 15:18-25. Then read John 15:26–16:15. What
> were the disciples going to face shortly after Jesus' death?
> Why do you think Jesus chose this moment to talk about
> the coming of the Holy Spirit?

> Why does verse 7 say Jesus must go away? How would this
> be a benefit to the disciples?

Jesus leaving the disciples was a good thing. Hard to believe, right? Jesus was with them for a short while, limiting Him in what He could do for them. However, the Holy Spirit would live within them forever. He would guide them into all truth because He is the truth. He could teach them from the inside out, not speaking on His own but speaking as One with God the Father and God the Son.

What did Jesus say the Holy Spirit would convict the world about (vv. 8-11)? And why?

1.

2.

3.

Part of His work is convicting the world of three things: sin, righteousness, and judgment. He convicts about sin so that we might repent and believe Jesus for salvation. No one is saved apart from the convicting and transforming work of the Holy Spirit. He convicts about righteousness because the world has a confused view of righteousness—do enough good and you're justified. But Scripture and the Spirit remind us that even when we're trying our best, "all our righteous acts are like filthy rags" before the Lord (Isa. 64:6, NIV).

Finally, the Spirit convicts about judgment. Similar to the wrong view of righteousness, the world's view of judgment can be distorted and twisted—right becomes wrong, wrong becomes right. But the Spirit makes clear that embracing the world's form of judgment is dangerous ground, because the source of false judgment—Satan—has already been judged and condemned. He may steal, kill, and destroy today, but his end has already been determined. Those who follow him will face the same fate.

What do verses 12-15 say about how and what the Holy Spirit will speak?

The Holy Spirit guides us into all truth. He will not lead us astray. He doesn't speak on His own but speaks what He hears from the Son. And the Son has the knowledge of the Father. This is the beauty of our faith in a triune God—all three Persons of the Trinity are united in their essence, and all are involved in guiding us to righteousness.

What would the world prefer you use as your guide rather than God's Word and the Holy Spirit?

Those who do not follow Jesus are led by things such as desires, money, experiences, fun, or other people. With those things in the lead, it's much easier to "follow your heart" or do whatever you see fit. You're not required to sacrifice or deny yourself. But that is not the way of the cross. God has called us to lay down our desires and pleasures to follow Him. This means the decisions we make and the convictions we hold may not make sense to others, but still we must obey.

The decisions we make and the convictions we hold may not make sense to others, but still we must obey.

Describe a time, event, or situation in which you were clearly led by the Holy Spirit.

The Spirit will always lead you in a way that glorifies God, makes you more like Jesus, and upholds God's Word. If faced with a choice that opposes God's Word, quickly dismiss it, or better yet, run in the opposite direction.

Of course, Scripture doesn't usually state specifically, "You should take this job" or "You should move to another city." However, the Holy Spirit will use Scripture to evaluate your motives, shape your desires, and change your thinking. Remember that the foremost way God speaks to you is through His Word. The Spirit will also use godly counsel, impressions in prayer, and circumstances to guide you, but the plumb line to measure all those against is the Word.

Being led by the Holy Spirit can feel a little nebulous at times, but one thing is for sure: As your walk with the Lord deepens, you will become more and more like the One you follow.

Are you currently being guided by the Holy Spirit? If not, why? If so, what is the evidence?

The Holy Spirit comforts and guides, transforming our hearts to live in the freedom Christ gives us.

The Holy Spirit comforts and guides, transforming our hearts to live in the freedom Christ gives us. He calls us to live holy lives and is the power through which we can obey.

The Spirit is not only at work in our individual lives. His role is "to manifest the active presence of God in the world, and especially in the church."[46]

How do you see the Holy Spirit at work in your church?

The Holy Spirit is working in you and the church to accomplish God's purposes in the world.

BUILDING YOUR THEOLOGY: Summarize today's key truth in 1–2 sentences.

LIVING YOUR THEOLOGY: How does this truth affect the way you live your everyday life?

PRAY: Thank God for sending the Holy Spirit to teach, guide, and correct you. Ask the Holy Spirit to convict you of any unconfessed or unrecognized sin in your life. Commit to following the guidance of the Spirit with a teachable heart.

MEDITATE AND MEMORIZE: John 14:26

THE HOLY SPIRIT IS THE KING'S SEAL ON OUR HEARTS

Review the spiritual blessings found in Ephesians 1:3-14. List some of them below:

One of the blessings of being in Jesus is knowing you were chosen by God. We can't understand this action, nor do we deserve it, but out of God's kindness and love He chose us for Himself. Scholars disagree on how election works, but what we can all affirm is that God choosing us before the foundation of the earth (Eph. 1:4) should humble us, move us to praise Him, and marvel at His love. All Persons of the Trinity are involved in the work of election.

According to verses 13-14, what is the Spirit's role in salvation?

The Holy Spirit is the down payment of the inheritance that is to come. (See also 2 Cor. 1:21-22.)

What is the purpose of a down payment?

Just as a down payment on a house is a small portion of what you promise to pay in full, the Holy Spirit is just a taste of the future glory we will experience in God's presence for all eternity.

The Holy Spirit is a seal on our hearts.

Seals were used as signatures in the ancient world. A seal would often be a symbol engraved on a ring worn by a king or powerful person. Letters, deeds, and edicts would be sealed by wax or clay with the signet ring pressed into it, leaving the imprint or signature on the document. Seals would also be used on wineskins or bottles of wine. A broken seal would make it obvious the wine had been poisoned or tampered with.

If your family had a seal, what would it look like? Draw it below.

A letter or container was forever changed when its seal was poured and stamped. The seal made the sender or owner instantly recognizable. When the Holy Spirit comes into our hearts, He isn't a tattoo on our skin that is visible for all the world to see. Instead, His stamp is Himself, present in our lives. The new life we have in Christ is initiated, sustained, and sealed by the Holy Spirit.

Read Esther 8:1-8. What did the king give Mordecai, Esther's cousin, and why?

What does the king say about an edict sealed with the royal signet ring in verse 8?

Haman sought the demise of the Jews, deceptively trying to snuff them out without the king's knowledge. Haman had an edict drawn up that all Jews were to be destroyed. The document was written in the king's name and sealed with the king's signet ring, so it was irrevocable. Yet Esther bravely went before the king to plead on behalf of God's people and was able to reveal Haman's plot. But because the first edict was irrevocable, Esther had to go back to the king for help, and another irrevocable edict was issued.

The seal of the Holy Spirit upon a believer's heart is irrevocable. Once you are born into the family of God, you remain there forever.

> How is your life different now that you have trusted in Jesus for salvation and been sealed with the Holy Spirit? Is His seal on you obvious to the world? Explain.

The seal of the Holy Spirit upon a believer's heart is irrevocable. Once you are born into the family of God, you remain there forever.

The Holy Spirit's seal on our hearts is our assurance that we will be saved eternally and will dwell and reign with Christ. However, His presence in your life may not always be as clear as a king's seal on an edict. This could lead to questions and doubt. In fact, many Christians deal with doubt at some point in their relationship with God. You may need to ask God some hard questions. There's nothing wrong with that. God is not intimidated by your struggle. In fact, Peter wrote, "Therefore, brothers and sisters, make every effort to confirm your calling and election" (2 Pet. 1:10a). The tense of the Greek word for "confirm" implies this is decisive action we need to do again and again.[47]

Wanting to make sure that you really do know Christ and are seeking to walk in obedience is part of the Holy Spirit's work.

> Do you ever struggle with doubt in your relationship with God? Do you ever worry that maybe your salvation didn't stick? Explain.

If you are doubting today, know that you aren't alone. I've talked with many Christians who are trusting Jesus and seeking to obey Him, confessing their sin, and yielding the fruit of the Holy Spirit's work in their lives, yet doubt still plagues them from time to time. Satan will lie to you and seek to quiet the Holy Spirit's work in your life. But the promise is this: If you have given your life to Jesus, the Holy Spirit is within you, and your salvation is sure.

However, if in your searching for certainty you realize you've never truly trusted in Christ for salvation, you have the opportunity to do that today. Repent of your sins and place your trust in the finished work of Christ for your salvation. Submit your life to Him in this moment.

The assurance of your salvation and commitment to God isn't something to be ignored but to be prayed through. You may also want to discuss this struggle with trusted godly friends.

> Spend some time reflecting on your relationship with Christ. Where do you find yourself in the journey?

Make sure of your standing with Christ. Eternity is at risk.

BUILDING YOUR THEOLOGY: Summarize today's key truth in 1–2 sentences.

LIVING YOUR THEOLOGY: How does this truth affect the way you live your everyday life?

PRAY: Thank God for giving you the Holy Spirit as the down payment, or guarantee, of eternal life with Him and abundant life on earth. Thank Him for being a God you can know and rest assured in.

MEDITATE AND MEMORIZE: 2 Corinthians 1:21-22

THE HOLY SPIRIT IS THE LIFE GIVER

Paul made it clear in Ephesians 2 that before we met Christ we were dead in our sins. As Ravi Zacharias put it, "Jesus does not offer to make bad people good but to make dead people alive."[48]

Read Romans 8:1-13. How is the Holy Spirit a life Giver?

Paul said those who live according to the flesh have their minds set on the flesh. Those who live for this world and the things of this world are focused on things that are hostile to God. That mind-set is death. But those who live by the Spirit have their minds set on God and the ways of God. That mind-set brings life and peace.

What does a mind that is set on the Spirit look like in everyday life?

Life throws some not-so-fun curveballs our way sometimes. But not a single one of them comes without God's knowledge and intention, and most of all, without His presence. Jesus promised a Counselor or Comforter to be with us in both the hardest times and the easiest times. The Holy Spirit is best for this job because He is God, He knows the intention and purpose of what we're walking through, and He lives within us.

What have we received through Jesus' work and the presence of the Holy Spirit in our hearts (Rom. 8:15-17)?

How should this change the way we live our lives?

Read Romans 8:18-27. What are the "sufferings of this present time" (v. 18) in your life?

This world is overwhelmingly broken. The sufferings of this world are a picture of our "bondage to decay" (v. 21) brought on by sin. But it will not always be this way.

Let's dream a little. What does your heart most yearn for that will be true after Jesus returns?

I'm not exactly sure what eternity will be like, but I'm looking forward to all vegetables tasting amazing, never having to fix my hair because I will always look radiant, and consuming whatever "coffee alternative" is available, knowing it will be a million times better than my beloved morning elixir. More than that, I cannot wait to look into the face of my Savior who endured such suffering so that I could have life, to worship Him and thank Him for the end of sadness and sickness, and to know Him as I have been known by Him.

Creation groans for this day. We who know Christ groan for it, knowing that the gift of the Holy Spirit is only the firstfruits of the goodness of eternity with our God!

What does it mean that the Spirit is our "firstfruits" (v. 23)?

In the Old Testament, the Israelites dedicated the firstfruits—the first harvested portion of the crops—to God for His faithfulness to provide for them. These were offered on the Sabbath day following the Passover feast (Lev. 23:9-14). It also signified the faith God's people had that the rest of the harvest would follow the first. The Holy Spirit as firstfruits is a picture of the promise that God will dwell with His people for eternity. It's just a little preview to the full-length experience of what it will be like when Jesus returns to rule and reign.

But the Holy Spirit is not just a promise for the future. He's here to help us now.

Have you ever been struck with such difficulty or suffering that you didn't even know how to pray? When?

When times are hard and we don't know what to pray, the Holy Spirit intercedes for us with words that are so deep they are incomprehensible to us.

How does the ministry of the Spirit in verses 26-27 comfort and encourage you?

My dad died of cancer when I was twelve. I remember being devastated. For five years I begged God to heal him. But when the healing came in a way that I didn't desire, I wasn't really sure what to pray. Suddenly, words failed. You've probably been there too.

When times are hard and we don't know what to pray, the Holy Spirit prays for us. Let that sink in. The Holy Spirit, who is one with God the Father and Jesus, intercedes for us with words that are so deep they are incomprehensible to us.

Read Romans 8:28-39. What is true of the believer who has been given life through the Holy Spirit?

What encouragement can you take with you for this week from this passage?

It's exciting and comforting to know that all things will be made right one day. No more suffering or shame. No more death or disease. Just eternal life, peace, and rejoicing with God our Savior. But it's also good to know that until that time comes, we are not left alone to stagger through the darkness. We have the Comforter to lead us, pray for us, sanctify us, and hold us. He gives us life, now and forever.

BUILDING YOUR THEOLOGY: Summarize today's key truth in 1–2 sentences.

LIVING YOUR THEOLOGY: How does this truth affect the way you live your everyday life?

PRAY: Thank God for giving you the Holy Spirit to be with you, guide you, and intercede for you.

MEDITATE AND MEMORIZE: Romans 8:26-27

THE HOLY SPIRIT CULTIVATES FRUIT

Last year, I took an interest in gardening. I bought twenty strawberry plants, three blueberry plants, and three packets of seeds: tomatoes, peppers, and spinach. I thought, *If I'm going to do this gardening thing, I'm going to do it right.* I looked up the right times to plant, the correct depth, and how often to water.

What I didn't research was how far apart to plant everything. It wasn't long before the tomato plants were growing on top of each other and the spinach was in a winner-takes-all battle with the leaves of the pepper plants. I had impossible-to-separate strawberry plants so tightly wound together I couldn't determine which limbs belonged to which roots.

I tried to weed out some of the angry overgrowth, but it only left the spinach subject to the scorching sun and the strawberries with hurt feelings. The baby blueberry bushes were the most promising, but they, too, hunched their backs in defeat. Months went by with no fruit. Most of the plants had the appearance of health. They were green and growing wildly, but they were not bearing fruit.

Sometimes we can look spiritually healthy but are actually far from bearing the fruit of the Spirit. This fruit is the measure of the work of the Holy Spirit in our hearts. He cultivates it, trimming the problematic parts from our hearts that are not growing as they should, and nourishes us with His Word. Unlike my gardening endeavor, the Spirit knows how His creation works best and how to produce abundant fruit.

Read Galatians 5:16-25. How would you define each fruit of the Spirit?

Love	
Joy	
Peace	
Patience	
Kindness	
Goodness	
Faithfulness	
Gentleness	
Self-control	

Thanks be to God, we can't muster these up on our own and aren't expected to. We might be able to fake them for a season but they won't last. Only our perfect Gardener, who tends to our soul, causes lasting fruit to grow. Jesus said it like this:

"I am the vine; you are the branches. The one who remains in me and I in him produces much fruit, because you can do nothing without me."
JOHN 15:5

Read Galatians 5:16-18 again. What does it mean to "walk by the Spirit" (v. 16)?

Walking by the Spirit is walking in freedom from the oppression of the Law or of needing to keep the Law to be right with God. Instead, we are free to follow because we love God and want to obey and please Him. It's not condemnation; it's blessing!

Read Galatians 5:1-6.

We often think of freedom as doing whatever we want. That's not what these verses are talking about. The Greek transliteration of the word for "freedom" is *eleutheria*, which is specifically regarding freedom from slavery.[49] We are no longer enslaved to sin and the consequences of the Law. Instead, we can live—or walk—by the Spirit. Today, the Law isn't our motivator as it may have been in the Old Testament. Instead, the Spirit and the life that He gives us is our motivator, and we live holy lives in response to His work in our hearts. We are now free to obey and joyfully follow Jesus.

The new sign of being a part of God's family isn't circumcision of the body but circumcision of the heart.

The context of this list of the fruit of walking in the Spirit and the fruit of walking in the flesh is a reminder of the Old Testament process of circumcision under the Abrahamic covenant.

Read Genesis 17:9-14. What was the point of circumcision?

God commanded His people to be set apart, and the outward sign was circumcision. Evidently, the Galatians were submitting again to this "yoke of slavery" (Gal. 5:1) by trying to obey the Law to earn favor with God. But the covenant that required obedience to the Law was no longer in effect. The Law, circumcision, and sacrifices could not earn salvation. Only a heart changed by the Holy Spirit could please God. Those seeking to be found righteous because of their outward show of faith would be found wanting.

The new sign of being a part of God's family isn't circumcision of the body but circumcision of the heart. The Holy Spirit's presence and production of fruit in our lives displays our status as children of God.

How do you see evidence of the fruit of the Spirit in your life?

Which characteristic of the fruit of the Spirit seems to be most difficult for you to bear? Why?

Just like I couldn't force my plants to grow, we cannot cultivate true fruit from our own lives, no matter how hard we try. Instead, the Holy Spirit's work in us causes the growth. We respond simply in obedience to the work He is doing in our hearts.

BUILDING YOUR THEOLOGY: Summarize today's key truth in 1–2 sentences.

LIVING YOUR THEOLOGY: How does this truth affect the way you live your everyday life?

PRAY: Ask God to cultivate fruit in your life through the Holy Spirit. Pray specifically about what attribute of the fruit of the Spirit can be a struggle for you. Thank God for sending the Holy Spirit to do the work that you couldn't do on your own.

MEDITATE AND MEMORIZE: Galatians 5:22-23

FURTHER STUDY: What other questions do you have about the Holy Spirit?

RESOURCES

THE WORK OF THE HOLY SPIRIT IN THE OLD AND NEW TESTAMENTS

OLD TESTAMENT

The Holy Spirit was active in the Old Testament but in different ways than in the New Testament. The first mention of Him is in Genesis 1:2, where we see Him "hovering over the surface of the waters."

The Holy Spirit guided prophets and authors of Scripture in the content of their messages, ultimately making Him the divine author of all the Bible (Num. 11:29; 2 Sam. 23:2; 2 Pet. 1:20-21).

We also see the Holy Spirit moving people to trust and obey God, including people outside the nation of Israel: Jethro the Midianite (Ex. 18), Rahab (Josh. 2), Ruth the Moabite (Ruth 1–4), and others.

He came upon kings and judges to give them special wisdom or extraordinary power like Joshua (Num. 27:18), Othniel (Judg. 3:10), Gideon (Judg. 6:34), and Saul (1 Sam. 10:9-10).[50]

NEW TESTAMENT

The Holy Spirit came upon Mary and she became pregnant (Matt. 1:18; Luke 1:35). He led Simeon to the temple to see the Messiah when Mary and Joseph brought Jesus to be dedicated (Luke 2:25-35).

He was certainly active in Jesus' life and ministry: descending upon Him at His baptism (Matt. 3:13-17), leading Jesus into the wilderness to be tempted (Matt. 4:1-11), empowering Jesus for ministry (Acts 10:38), and ultimately raising Jesus from the dead (Rom. 8:11).

In the church age after Pentecost we have a more full experience of His presence, as He lives within those who follow Christ. He illuminates Scripture, unveils our sin, and moves us to trust Jesus. He empowers us, comforts us, and intercedes for us. He also gives every believer spiritual gifts for service in the church.

SPIRITUAL GIFTS

Romans 12:3-8 is a great reminder that every person who trusts Jesus is given spiritual gifts from the Holy Spirit. These gifts are to be used for the edification of the church, not for our own applause. When we aren't using our gifts, the church suffers. (For more biblical information on gifts, read 1 Cor. 12–14.)

What are the gifts of the Spirit?
Gifts of the Spirit are "manifestation[s] of the Spirit" (1 Cor. 12:7), so they are absolutely supernatural. Thomas Schreiner lists the gifts named in the New Testament (although there could be others) as apostleship, prophecy, evangelism, discernment (able to distinguish between spirits), teaching (including wisdom and knowledge), exhortation, miracles, healing, service, leadership/administration, tongues (and interpreting them), giving, faith, and mercy. (Apostleship is sometimes used to refer to those who followed Jesus directly [the disciples, Paul, James], but others use it to describe pioneering missionaries [Rom. 16:7]).

Have miraculous gifts ceased (tongues, miracles, prophecy, healing)?
There are two streams of thought here. The continuationists believe the miraculous gifts are still being manifested today and will continue to be until Christ's return. The cessationists believe these gifts ended with the apostolic age. [51]

We need to keep in mind that while this debate is important, it is not central to the gospel. There are faithful, godly followers of Christ on both sides of this issue.

(More information on spiritual gifts is found in Session 7.)

FAQS

What is blasphemy of the Holy Spirit?
Matthew 12:31-32 calls it the unforgivable sin. Blaspheming the Holy Spirit
means taking a continual and hardened stance against God. Pastor J. D. Greear
says it like this: "We all have moments, even sustained periods of our lives, when
we defy God. But there may come a point in a person's life when that becomes
an unyielding defiance against God and he or she refuses to let the Spirit speak.
... Or to put it another way, the only unpardonable sin is refusing to let God
pardon you."[52]

What is the baptism of the Spirit/filling of the Holy Spirit?
R. C. Sproul says this "is the work of the Spirit upon a human being to endow
that person with the power necessary to carry out their mission and vocation as
a Christian."[53] This is an experience that happens at the moment of regeneration. We could also speak of it as the indwelling of the Spirit. When Paul spoke
of being "filled by the Spirit" in Ephesians 5:18, he was not referring to the
baptism or indwelling experience that equips a believer for ministry. Rather he
was talking about "having an awareness, a keen awareness and consciousness,
of the powerful presence of the Spirit."[54]

Is being "slain in the Spirit" biblical?
Could the Holy Spirit move so powerfully that people fall over at the force of His
power? Sure. However, we don't see any examples of this in the New Testament,
and this isn't what happened at Pentecost when we see a clear picture of the
power of the Spirit.

What does it mean to grieve the Holy Spirit (Eph. 4:30)?
The Persons of the Trinity are just that, Persons. They have perfect emotions.
Kevin DeYoung describes grieving the Holy Spirit as, "refusing to see and to
savor what the Spirit means to show us."[55] We grieve the Holy Spirit when we
disregard Him by willfully sinning against Him or misrepresenting Him (like
saying He's leading us to do something counter to Scripture).

GROUP TIME

OPEN

Begin your group time with the large group discussing the following questions:

What was the highlight of your week of study?

What was something new you learned this week?

How did this week's study challenge what you believe about the Holy Spirit?

REVIEW AND DISCUSS

Break into smaller groups to complete this section. Use the following Scripture passages and questions to review what you learned in your personal Bible study on the Holy Spirit.

Read John 14:15-17.
How is the Holy Spirit described in this passage? What personally resonates with you? Why?

Why do you think there is so much misunderstanding about the person and work of the Spirit?

Read John 16:7-15.
Explain the work of the Spirit described in this passage.

How do you see the Spirit doing this work in your life?

Read Ephesians 1:13-14.
Explain the Holy Spirit's role in our salvation according to this passage.

How does being sealed with the Spirit help you have assurance of your salvation?

Read Romans 8:6-11.
What's the difference between a person whose mind is set on the flesh versus set on the Spirit?

What part of the Spirit's work described in Romans 8 speaks to you most deeply?

Read Galatians 5:16-25.
What does it mean to walk in the Spirit and be led by the Spirit?

How do you see the fruit of the Spirit manifested in your life?

REFLECT AND APPLY

Spend a moment writing your answers to the following questions, then discuss with your small group.

What other questions about the Holy Spirit did this week's study raise?

What's your main takeaway from this study on the Holy Spirit?

Why does what you believe about the Holy Spirit matter?

Is the Spirit fully in control of your life? If not, why? If so, what is the evidence?

CLOSE

Share stories together of how you are seeing the Holy Spirit work in your life, family, and church. Close with a time of praise and gratefulness for His work.

HUMANITY

SESSION 5

YOU ARE CREATED IN GOD'S IMAGE

The sun shone brightly and the stars twinkled in their constellations, shifting slowly across the sky. I have to wonder if the lions curled up with the zebras to sleep, and the snakes rode on the backs of skunks, enjoying their sweet smell. Vegetation grew wildly, and fruit was never overtaken by weeds. The water was crystal clear and teemed with the most beautiful fish. All of this and God still had not completed His most amazing work.

> Read Genesis 1:26-31. Write the first phrase that God said in verse 26. What truth does this phrase reveal?

As we've discussed in other sessions, God the Father didn't create alone. We are made in the image of our triune God, and each Person was involved in the creation of man.

> How was the creation of humans different from God's past work of creation? (Revisit Gen. 1:1-26 if needed.)

God could have created humans in the image of something He had already created, but instead He created us in His own image.

> What do you think it means to be created in God's image?

In *Created in God's Image*, Anthony R. Hoekema discusses the Hebrew words for *image* and *likeness,* noting that *tselem* (image) is derived from "to carve,"

*Then God said,
"Let us make man
in our image,
according to our
likeness."*

GENESIS 1:26

as a carved likeness of an animal or person, and *demuth* (likeness) indicates "an image which is like us."[56] God chose to make us like Him in both form and image. You are both a picture of God and a representative of God on earth. That feels like a big responsibility, right?

How are humans both a picture and representative of God?

What makes a person a person?

The second question seems like a simple one, but it is not without debate. Consider debates on abortion, slavery, or how countries have been led to genocide. What makes a person a person matters.

A person is made up of a body and a soul and/or spirit. Although there are disagreements over whether we are body and soul (dichotomy) or body, soul, and spirit (trichotomy), we can agree we are a unity of the material (body) and the immaterial (soul/spirit), and God created both good and with purpose.

Scholars also disagree about exactly where the image of God is seen in humanity. Some say it's found in our intellect or our ability to reason. Others say it's our morality, our status as spiritual beings, our ability to have relationships with God and with each other, or our functional dominion over all the earth.

Yet it seems we reflect God in all of these aspects. Imperfectly, of course. Still, being made in His image makes us different from all of creation and makes every human life worthy of dignity.

How does this inform the way God sees us? The way we should see ourselves? The way we should see others?

When we view creation through God's eyes, every person has infinite worth. They are eternal beings, just like you. We are to love them as God loves them, and we are to love ourselves as God loves us, even when they (or we) are difficult to love.

Maybe you find your body hard to love. It may not currently do what you want or look like you want. But all God created is good. Sin has depraved us, but it has not removed God's image from us. And for Christians, His image is progressively becoming clearer in each of us as we continue in the process of _sanctification_, or being made more like Him (Rom. 8:29; 2 Cor. 3:18).

What responsibility did God give the first humans (Gen. 1:28)?

This instruction is often called the cultural mandate. Bearing God's image comes with responsibilities to be fruitful and multiply: building societies and filling the earth with God's glory, and reigning over all creation and stewarding it well. The work reflects the character of God, but it is also reliant upon the Lord to yield fruit.

Read Ephesians 2:8-10. How are you described in verse 10?

You are infinitely valuable and worthy of dignity, not because of what you do, but because you are made in God's image.

This passage should be the battle cry against the feeling that you are unimportant. You are God's "workmanship." His "masterpiece" (NLT). The Greek word for "workmanship" is *poiema*, from where we get our word *poem*.[57] Making you was not just about effort; it also involved artistic skill and craftsmanship. You are infinitely valuable and worthy of dignity, not because of what you do, but because you are made in God's image. And there is valuable work that He has purposed you to do.

How are you stewarding your life and what God has given you dominion over (your things, your work, your family) for God's glory?

Read Revelation 7:9-12. Describe the scene below.

Every tribe, nation, ethnicity, and personality type was created by God. He chose the beautiful colors of our skin and the languages of our mouths. God created a people for Himself that is incredibly diverse, and one day all of His people will sing His praises together. We have more in common with the person who loves Jesus but is completely different from us than we do with someone who shares our DNA but is far from Christ.

Have you harbored wrong attitudes, taken wrong actions, or spoken hurtful words against other image-bearers you need to confess before God? Who do you need to contact to seek forgiveness for your thoughts and behavior?

BUILDING YOUR THEOLOGY: Summarize today's key truth in 1–2 sentences.

LIVING YOUR THEOLOGY: How does this truth affect the way you live your everyday life?

PRAY: Ask God to help you see yourself and others in His image. Seek His forgiveness if you've judged others as less than. Ask for help to see people through His eyes.

MEDITATE AND MEMORIZE: Genesis 1:26

YOU ARE CREATED MALE OR FEMALE

When I was in middle school I thought finding your spouse meant finding the man whose rib matched yours (obviously revealing you had been taken from his side and were to be his wife). I'm not sure how I would know when I found him. I guess I thought an X-ray at the local hospital was required before saying yes to his proposal of marriage. (Yes, I seriously believed this.)

What I didn't know is ribs look shockingly similar. Also, I had completely missed the point of the creation story in Genesis 1–2.

   Read Genesis 1:26–2:25.

It may seem unusual that both Genesis 1 and Genesis 2 record the creation of Adam and Eve. However, based on ancient writings from around the same time, stating and restating with more detail was a normal literary style of recording history. The two accounts aren't two separate creations. Instead, as *The New American Commentary* states, it seems "verse 2:4a repeats the same information as 1:1 and therefore ties 1:1–2:3 and 2:4b–4:26 together; both passages recount first things, but the second narrative goes beyond the first by tracking the story of Adam's family."[58]

   Why did God create Eve?

This act of creation reveals God's desire and ability to perfectly meet our needs. Adam needed a helper, so God met the need with someone like him but also different from him. It's in these differences that the whole of humanity is better at revealing God's character than an individual.

God could have filled this need by speaking Eve into existence or creating her from dust as He did Adam, but instead He made her from Adam's rib.

We are just speculating here, but why do you think the way Eve was made is significant?

From creation, we see God's intention for man and woman to be different. He created gender.

Read the following passages and note what phrase is repeated.

Genesis 1:27; 5:2

Matthew 19:4

Mark 10:6

God made the man then the woman. Distinct. Different. But He also made them one through the institute of marriage. There is a closeness and rightness of relationship. The order of creation is not a hierarchy of value, as both man and woman are equally loved and equally made in the image of God, even in their differences. God placed Adam in the garden to "work it and watch over it" (Gen. 2:15). He was given the responsibility to provide and protect. Then God noted it was not good for man to be alone, so He created Eve.

What word is used to describe Eve in Genesis 2:18?

The word translated "helper" is 'ezer in Hebrew.[59] This word does not denote a subservient assistant. Instead, it is even used to describe God in the Old Testament, as in Psalm 121:1-2: "I lift my eyes toward the mountains. Where will my help [`ezer] come from? My help [`ezer] comes from the LORD, the Maker of heaven and earth."

"Helper" indicates importance and aid. Both man and woman were needed and valuable, a complement to the other and a clearer view of God's image together.

Before the fall, marriage was good and beautiful in all ways. All relationships among people were respectful and caring, a reflection of the love and care God has for us. Genesis 1 and 2 reveal the perfect picture of humanity's relationship with each other, with the rest of the world, and with God.

What does Genesis 2:18-25 tell us is true about marriage?

In terms of marriage, one man and one woman would be joined together as one flesh for all of life, able to better serve God together than apart. There are biological implications that echo this idea of complementing. In marriage, the husband is to love His wife sacrificially, dying to himself, and leading her as Christ leads and loves the church (Eph. 5:22-33). The wife is to submit to the husband's leadership, and husbands and wives are also to submit to one another, valuing one another because they are made in the image of God and are of immeasurable value to Him.

What does the Genesis passage mean for people who are single? Are they a lesser picture of God's image because of their singleness? Explain.

Both man and woman were needed and valuable, a complement to the other and a clearer view of God's image together.

Jesus was the perfect man, yet He was not married. Paul also said it was good to be single. Obviously this is not a statement about what is good and right for everyone. If you are single, you have capacities to be engaged deeply in ministry in a way that a married couple cannot. Whether called to marriage or to singleness, the call is the same: to die to self and clearly show the world Jesus.

How does the Genesis passage inform our view of sex according to God's design? How does it challenge popular views about sex today?

In a world where any view that doesn't embrace non-binary gender is deemed archaic and unfair, this passage is a helpful reminder of God's intention in creation and the purpose for creating as He did. God's design before sin entered the world was good and right.

Dying to self is grueling work, but God calls us to holiness.

However, that doesn't give us freedom to be unkind to those dealing with the struggle of sexual sin or gender confusion. Remember, all are made in the image of God, and all struggle against temptation. Our temptations and struggles with sin are probably not the same. However, we can all be sympathetic to the process. Dying to self is grueling work, but God calls us to holiness. God created all things purposefully, and we are to live within His design. He created us male and female to bring Him glory.

BUILDING YOUR THEOLOGY: Summarize today's key truth in 1–2 sentences.

LIVING YOUR THEOLOGY: How does this truth affect the way you live your everyday life?

PRAY: Thank God for creating man and woman in His image, and for creating you uniquely and beautifully. Ask Him to strengthen you as you live out His purpose.

MEDITATE AND MEMORIZE: Genesis 1:27

DAY 3

YOU ARE SINFUL

My mom deserves all the jewels in her crown. I exited the womb knowing how to rebel, often in subtle but unbelievably stubborn ways. She didn't have to teach me to yell or sling things at my brother or to grunt at her when I didn't get my way. I was an expert at all of the above.

I'm not the only one who inherited Adam's bent toward sin. Sin afflicts all of us. Romans 5:12 says, "Therefore, just as sin came into the world through one man, and death through sin, and so death spread to all men because all sinned" (ESV). (More on this in Ps. 51:5; Rom. 3:23; 5:13-14,18-19.)

> Read Genesis 3:1-24. What was God's prohibition about the tree of the knowledge of good and evil (Gen. 2:16-17)? How was it different from what Eve told the serpent?

> What did the serpent say to Eve to convince her to eat of the fruit?

Ultimately, Adam and Eve's sin was a result of unbelief. They were deceived into believing God had not told them the truth, that He was holding out on them. They doubted His faithfulness to care for them and give them His very best. They were convinced their will was better than His will. Unbelief is always the root of sin.

> Do you agree with that last statement? Why or why not?

We sin because we don't believe God is God. We don't believe He is wise, sovereign, good, and faithful. We don't trust Him. We choose our own way, our own reasoning. For example, we struggle with pride because we don't believe God is in control, or that His control is much better than ours could ever be.

What is sin? Define it below.

I like to define *sin* as anything we think, do, or say that is against God's instructions in the Bible, or anything we don't think, do, or say, but should. It's missing the mark of God's perfect holiness, a selfish rebellion and transgression against Him. By nature, we do not want to obey God on our own.

I want to make a god of myself and do what I want when and how I want. It is only through God's work in my life that I believe dying to these selfish desires is good because God is good. Although we've been forgiven and freed from bondage to sin through Christ, we can still struggle with it. Some sin may be a struggle for a season, or one particular sin might plague you for a large portion of your life. The writer of Hebrews called it "the sin that so easily ensnares us" (Heb. 12:1). It could be gossip, pride, an obsession with what people think of you, disordered eating, sexual sin, or a multitude of other things. However, God's right desire is that we put it to death.

What sin(s) do you struggle with? What sin so easily ensnares you? Is there a pattern of sin that you need to put to death today? Explain.

What is it that you are not believing about God when you fall to these sins?

In the garden, Satan cast doubt on God's goodness and lied about the consequences of sin. He continues to use the same tactics today. He intends to steal, kill, and destroy lives by making sin sound fun and exciting, only for us to realize that the consequences of sin are more costly than we ever imagined.

> Read the list of consequences for Adam and Eve's sin in Genesis 3:16-19. What consequences have you faced as a result of sin?

> How do most people view sin in our culture? How does Scripture tell us it must be viewed?

Sin is serious, and without Jesus setting us free, we are enslaved to it. It separates us from God because He is holy and righteous and cannot be in the presence of sin. Adam and Eve's sin didn't surprise God. He wasn't shocked, and He didn't scramble to figure out a plan B. In the same breath that God made it clear sin required punishment, He also promised He would one day send someone who would crush the serpent's head (3:15). That someone was Jesus.

> Why would God create people who would rebel?

In the garden, Satan cast doubt on God's goodness and lied about the consequences of sin. He continues to use the same tactics today.

Scripture doesn't tell us the answers to all of our questions, but we can trust that having the ability to sin and the ability to choose to obey God instead is designed to bring Him glory and honor. We are not robots forced to obey. Instead, we obey out of love.

> Revisit Genesis 3:21. How do we see God's kindness to Adam and Eve?

The consequences of sin are difficult to swallow, but the kindness of God is visible at every turn. One of the many consequences of Adam and Eve's sin was noticing their nakedness and the shame it brought them. God kindly relieved this consequence by slaughtering an animal and clothing them. This first sacrifice foreshadowed God's future kindness through the sacrifice of His Son.

How has God shown kindness to you despite your sin?

From the beginning, sin has wreaked havoc in our world. Adam and Eve's choice condemned us and implanted a bent toward sin that we willfully choose to follow, thus condemning ourselves. But God, rich in mercy and grace, because of His great love for us, has made a way. More about that in the days to come.

BUILDING YOUR THEOLOGY: Summarize today's key truth in 1–2 sentences.

LIVING YOUR THEOLOGY: How does this truth affect the way you live your everyday life?

PRAY: Spend some time confessing your sin to God. Thank Him for sending Jesus to pay for sin, and that His plan was always to redeem His people.

MEDITATE AND MEMORIZE: Romans 6:23

DAY 4

YOU ARE LOVED BY GOD DESPITE YOUR SIN

Having grown up in the church and in a Christian home, I can't remember a time I didn't know God loves me, at least in my head. Then my huband and I brought home a son of our own, and it was like I understood the love of God in the gospel message anew. God sent His Son to pay the penalty we deserved. This is the ultimate act of love.

We know love because God is love (1 John 4:8). All of His character and His ways are loving. His ultimate love poured out for us in Jesus. John 15:13 says, "No one has greater love than this: to lay down his life for his friends." We love God because He loved us first. We see His love, even when we sin, in His provision of relief from sin's consequences.

Read John 3:1-21. Why did Nicodemus come to Jesus?

What did Jesus tell Nicodemus he must do to be saved and see the kingdom of God?

Nicodemus was a Pharisee, which made him a top teacher of the Hebrew Scriptures in Israel. Yet he called Jesus "Rabbi" (Teacher) and sought to learn from Him. We don't know much about Nicodemus after this encounter, but it seems that he believed in Jesus since he later defended Him in John 7:50-52.

In John 3:1-21, Jesus used a story Nicodemus probably taught often from Numbers 21:4-9. This story was not a crowning moment for the Israelites.

Read Numbers 21:4-9. How did God show love in this passage?

Snakes. God sent snakes. If this isn't my worst-nightmare consequence for sin, I don't know what is. They weren't the kind of snakes that are "more afraid of you than you are of them" either. Eventually, God provided relief, but the Israelites had to trust Him to receive it.

This may seem like a strange story to discuss as a primary example of God's love, but it beautifully shows God's care for His people in the midst of their sin. God didn't remove the consequences of their sin, but the ultimate consequence—death—was withheld. God, in His graciousness, set a pattern for His people of what was to come. He would send His Son to be placed upon a cross, and all who turn from their sin and look upon Him—trusting Him as Savior and Lord—will be saved. Not from earthly death but from eternal death.

Write John 3:16 below.

Underline God's actions in the verse. Circle your action in this verse. Put a big square around the words that describe what those who trust Jesus will receive.

Read John 3:16-21 again. Why did God send His Son?

What does this passage say will be true of those who trust Jesus?

This passage is very familiar to most people. Even those who are far from God probably have some familiarity with it. But don't let your familiarity with it keep you from grasping the depth of it. We deserved death for our sin, and yet Jesus, God's Son, didn't come to condemn us for our sin. Instead, He came to liberate us from it! This is the lavishness of the love of God: that He didn't give us what we deserve but made a way for us to be His children.

This is the lavishness of the love of God: that He didn't give us what we deserve but made a way for us to be His children.

Rewrite verses 16 and 17 in your own words below.

What portion of this account of God's love is most dear to your heart?

Read Psalm 86:15. Write this verse in your own words as a prayer to God below.

This psalm worships God well for the way He loves His children. God's love for His people is ultimately seen in sending Jesus to pay our penalty for sin. As Paul said,

> "But God proves his own love for us in that while we were still sinners, Christ died for us!"
> **ROMANS 5:8**

God shows His patience in waiting to send Jesus back to earth so that more might believe (2 Pet. 3:9). We see His love in His compassion and grace, in His slowness to anger, in His faithfulness, and in His giving us truth.

In what ways have you seen God's love, mercy, and graciousness in your life?

No one is outside of God's love, and no one is incapable of receiving His forgiveness.

We see God's love from the very beginning to the very end of Scripture. He established covenants with His people because He loves them. He delivered His people out of Egypt because He loves them. He even disciplined them in the wilderness because He loves them. And He loves you and will keep His promises to you through Christ to deliver you from sin and death, to save you for eternity. No one is too lost or too sinful for Him to love and to save. He doesn't love you because you can do anything for Him but because you are His creation. No one is outside of His love, and no one is incapable of receiving His forgiveness.

"As the bridegroom rejoices over the bride, so shall your God rejoice over you."
ISAIAH 62:5, ESV

God *rejoices* over you. You bring Him glory when you find your joy, contentment, and purpose in Him.

How does your life look differently when you live in this truth?

BUILDING YOUR THEOLOGY: Summarize today's key truth in 1–2 sentences.

LIVING YOUR THEOLOGY: How does this truth affect the way you live your everyday life?

PRAY: Thank God for His good gift in providing Jesus. Spend some time praising Him for choosing to love you despite your sin.

MEDITATE AND MEMORIZE: Psalm 86:15

YOU ARE FREE THROUGH JESUS

Read Ephesians 2:1-22 and complete the chart below.

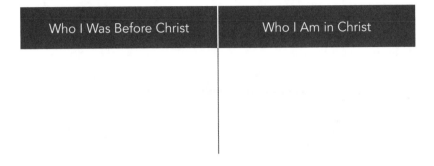

Who I Was Before Christ	Who I Am in Christ

What does verse 3 say about who we were before knowing Jesus?

Look up *wrath* in a dictionary. Write the definition that makes the most sense in this context.

"Children under wrath." These are not light words. But the best part about Ephesians 2 is the tense in which death and this identity as children under wrath are discussed. When we trust Jesus, our old self is crucified with Christ, and now, because of His resurrection, we can walk in new life, no longer bound by sin (Rom. 6:4-7). We were dead in our sins, but when we trust Jesus, we are made alive in Him, and the hold sin has on our lives is broken.

Write Ephesians 2:4-5 below.

Underline who is doing the action in these verses. Circle the "why" of this action. Put a box around what He has made true of us who trust Him for salvation.

But God. This tiny conjunctive statement changes everything. He is the reason we are not who we once were. He is the reason we are no longer dead in our sins, eternally condemned. He rescued us from the pit of despair by His mighty hand alone. This doesn't say, "But Mary strived and pulled herself up by her bootstraps." No, I was *dead*, and God raised me to new life by His unmerited favor through Christ's victory over sin, and He will raise me to glory when He returns. Christian, this truth is the same for you. Your identity is changed. You are not who you were.

There are plenty of things to find our identity in, but ultimately, we are defined by our relationship to Christ.

How would you describe yourself? What is the core of your identity?

Revisit Ephesians 2:8-10. What does this passage say about our identity and what we are to live for?

You may be a college student, mom, coworker, daughter, the best cook, shortstop, or gardener. (I'm none of those last three things, but more power to you if you are!) There are plenty of things to find our identity in, but ultimately, we are defined by our relationship to Christ. We are hidden in Him and made right with God because of His goodness to us.

We also may be fragile, limited, needy, and dependent, altogether excellent at raising up idols for ourselves, but in Christ we are also saints, temples of the Holy Spirit, empowered to do what He has called us to do through Him.

We can be dependent because He is the ultimate Provider. We can need sleep because He is always in control. We can be weak because He is strong. He's also perfectly excellent at tearing our idols down. This is love: not just that He does good things for us, but that He calls us to obedience, which is our greatest good. He has given us a new identity of being found in Him alone.

The Ephesians were once identified as "the uncircumcised" (2:11). They were not part of God's people, but they "have been brought near by the blood of Christ" (v. 13). Jesus changed their identity, removing the curse of the Law and bringing peace.

Your identity is not found in your circumstances. It's not in the difficult relationship you've suffered with a family member, the addiction you battle, or the crushing loss you've experienced. These moments do shape you, but they do not define you.

What else might you be tempted to place your identity in?

Your identity is not primarily mom, wife, coworker, or friend. Your identity is one who has union with Christ in His life, death, and resurrection, and you are free!

This fact squashes ungodly ambition, realigns your priorities, and liberates you to live a life free of others' expectations. It releases you from trying to find fulfillment in a relationship or in your job. It keeps you from putting undue pressure on other people around you because you need to find yourself in what they have to offer.

What does Ephesians 2:16-17 say Jesus put to death?

Our peace has a name: Jesus. Jesus not only put to death the hostility between God and man, He also put to death any hostility that divides us from each other. He has destroyed any divisions—racial, economic, social, cultural—and brought us together in Him.

God has brought us near. His heart has always been that we'd be in His presence—every tribe, tongue, and nation.

How does this passage speak to our prejudices? How does it change the way we view and relate to those who are different than us?

When we realize we are no longer enslaved to sin, we can live in freedom. Freedom to love God with all our hearts and freedom to love our neighbors as ourselves. Freedom in Christ is victory!

"So if the Son sets you free, you really will be free."
JOHN 8:36

BUILDING YOUR THEOLOGY: Summarize today's key truth in 1–2 sentences.

LIVING YOUR THEOLOGY: How does this truth affect the way you live your everyday life?

PRAY: Thank God for making you free from the crushing weight of sin, fear, and death and giving you life, joy, and security in Him!

MEDITATE AND MEMORIZE: Romans 8:1-2

FURTHER STUDY: What other questions do you have about what God says about you?

RESOURCE
SEXUAL ETHICS

SEX, MONOGAMY, AND FAITHFULNESS

God's design for sex is framed within the covenantal relationship of one woman and one man in marriage (Gen. 2:24). The intention is that the marital covenant will not be broken. God's negative view of divorce seems clear in Scripture (Matt. 19:1-9). However, there are situations in which Scripture allows divorce, including abandonment or unfaithfulness.

Sex outside of marriage is not God's design. Marriage is a picture of God's love for His people, and engaging in any sexual immorality is an untrue picture of the goodness of the gospel and a distortion of God's design. Sexual immorality (*porneia* in Greek, 1 Thess. 4:3) has consequences that could be physical, spiritual, and/or emotional, and although God's grace doesn't remove earthly consequences, it does remove condemnation, shame, and guilt.[60]

ABUSE

There is never a situation in which abuse is acceptable. Abuse can also fall under abandonment as grounds for divorce, because the home has become unsafe and the spouse has been abandoned emotionally and spiritually. If you are in a situation where you are being abused, please contact authorities immediately, get to a safe place, and reach out to a safe friend, family member, church leader, and/or counselor for support.

HOMOSEXUALITY AND TRANSGENDERISM

Homosexuality goes against God's design for human flourishing—one man, one woman in covenantal marriage. Paul's statement in 1 Thessalonians 4 and other passages of Scripture (Rom. 1:18-32; 1 Cor. 6:9-11) prohibit same-sex sexual relations. Transgenderism is similar, in that it goes against God's design for humanity (Rom. 1:26-28; 1 Cor. 6:9-11,17-20; 1 Tim. 1:8-11; Jude 5-8).

Believers who struggle against same-sex attraction should not describe themselves or embrace an identity that affirms sinful desires or the current culture's view on sex. Instead, they, like all of us who struggle against sin, should live in the grace of God that gives us pardon and power to no longer be enslaved to sin but walk in a manner worthy of the gospel (Rom. 6:1-14; 1 Cor. 10:13).

We need to encourage, minister to, and show Christlike love to those experiencing same-sex attraction.[61]

This may not be your struggle, but you can understand the experience of struggling with sin and seeking to rest your identity in Christ alone.

PORNOGRAPHY

Pornography is shockingly "mainstream" in churches today. Recently, the following statistics were reported:

- 47 percent of families in the United States report porn as a problem in their home.
- 68 percent of church-going men and over 50 percent of pastors view porn on a regular basis.
- 76 percent of Christians ages 18–24 actively search for porn.[62]

Many of the verses we've already mentioned speak to the sinfulness of pornography, especially 1 Thessalonians 4:3. We also need to hear the psalmist's call: "I will not set before my eyes anything that is worthless" (Ps. 101:3, ESV).

Despite the destruction these sexual sins can cause, none of them is unpardonable. All are covered by the blood of Christ if one repents and turns from their sinful behavior. I pray the church will be a safe place to discuss struggles like these, and that we'll be people who walk alongside those who are facing these temptations.

FAQS

Will we continue to sin after we become Christians?
When we come to Christ we are given a new nature; the old is gone, the new has come (2 Cor. 5:17). However, we still live in fleshly bodies that are bent toward sin. This will be a constant struggle until we see Jesus (Rom. 7:14-25). Fortunately, we have the promise that "if we confess our sins, he is faithful and righteous to forgive us our sins and to cleanse us from all unrighteousness" (1 John 1:9).

If the preceding paragraph is true, then what about 1 John 3:9, which says, "No one who is born of God will continue to sin, because God's seed remains in them; they cannot go on sinning, because they have been born of God" (NIV)? This verse doesn't mean that we won't sin, but the Holy Spirit won't allow us to happily continue sinning for long without driving us toward repentance. Also, sin's power is broken over us, so we have the ability to stand against temptation through the power of the Holy Spirit (Rom. 6:6-14).

What about other created things like angels, demons, and Satan?
Gregg Allison summarizes it this way, "Angels are highly intelligent, morally good, spiritual beings created by God. Some of the angels rebelled against God, lost their original goodness, and now as demons (with Satan as their head) attempt to combat God and his work."[63]

Is being rich/poor an illustration of what God thinks about us?
Our life situations are not necessarily a reflection of God's favor or of a person's level of faithfulness. However, the law of the harvest found in Galatians 6:7 does exist: "For whatever a person sows he will also reap." Sin does bear consequences. But for the most part, our lot in life is not directly related to the level of our sinfulness. We could say that generally all poverty, sickness, and sadness are caused by sin's presence in the world but not on an individual basis. We aren't told why God gives different situations to different people, but we can trust that God is just, good, and trustworthy. And as Paul told us in Romans 8:28, "All things work together for the good of those who love God, who are called according to His purpose."

GROUP TIME

OPEN

Begin your group time with the large group discussing the following questions:

What was the highlight of your week of study?

What was something new you learned this week?

How did this week's study challenge what you believe about humanity?

REVIEW AND DISCUSS

Break into smaller groups to complete this section. Use the following Scripture passages and questions to review what you learned in your personal Bible study on humanity.

Read Genesis 1:26-27.
What does it mean to be made in the image of God?

Do you ever struggle to see all people as made in God's image? Explain.

Read Genesis 2:15-18.
How did the Lord make man and woman distinct and different?

How has the world distorted God's design? What can we do to help them see the truth?

Read Romans 5:12.
How did sin enter the world? What was the tragic and lingering effect?

How does culture's view of sin differ from the biblical view? What happens if we lose sight of God's view of sin?

Read John 3:16-17.
How do these verses capture the heart of the gospel?

How have you personally experienced the lavish love of God?

Read Ephesians 2:14-15.
What does it mean to be free in Christ?

How has Jesus broken down the wall of hostility between us and God
and between each other?

REFLECT AND APPLY

Spend a moment writing your answers to the following questions, then discuss
with your small group.

What other questions about humanity did this week's study raise?

What's your main takeaway from this study on humanity?

Why does what you believe about humanity matter?

How has the study this week changed the way you view your
relationship with God? Your relationship with others?

CLOSE

Take time together to praise and thank God for breaking down the wall of
hostility and reconciling you to Himself through Christ. Then honestly consider
walls still present between you and others. Pray for healing, changed mind-sets,
forgiveness, and whatever needs to happen to see reconciliation take place.

SALVATION

SESSION 6

SALVATION IS A MIRACULOUS GIFT OF GOD

Imagine going to the mailbox and finding a package from a friend. She's sent you a gift! Then, as you shuffle through the junk mail, you find a medical bill that's going to be tough to pay. Describe the difference in the emotions you would feel.

We're going to start with a passage we looked at last week: Ephesians 2.

Write Ephesians 2:8-9 below, underlining the phrases that resonate most with you.

We sometimes live as if salvation depends on our goodness or good deeds. We check off the right number of hours reading the Bible, never forget to pray before a meal, stay away from "the big sins," and we think we've made it. After all, we aren't as bad as the next guy, right? But this passage reminds us we cannot achieve our own salvation. If we could, God wouldn't need to be gracious and kind. He could simply fulfill His duty as an employer to pay His employee. But if our salvation could be earned, we'd still fail at achieving it because we could never be righteous enough to please a holy God.

Salvation is totally a gift from God. In His power He regenerates us, giving us a new nature. We are born again, beginning our new life in Christ.

Read Colossians 1:21-23. Write the dictionary definition of *reconcile*.

How does this passage say we have we been reconciled? (See also Rom. 5:6-11.)

Jesus died the death we deserved so that we might be reconciled to God, presented to Him holy, faultless, and blameless.

What is the purpose of this reconciliation (v. 22)?

Before we came to Christ, we were hostile toward God. We were His enemies, estranged from Him and dead in our sin. Mercifully, God's unchanging love doesn't fail. Jesus died the death we deserved so that we might be reconciled to God, presented to Him holy, faultless, and blameless.

Reread verse 23. What might cause someone to shift away from the hope of the gospel?

Does this mean you could lose your salvation?

As we learned in Session 4, the Holy Spirit is a seal on our hearts proving that we belong to the Lord, and His presence in our lives assures us of our salvation. Paul's statement here was not a warning but rather an exhortation. Paul was encouraging them to continue in the faith, knowing that the true believers would. The Greek word for "if" used here could also be translated "since," making this an expression of confidence, not doubt.[64]

Read Titus 3:1-10.

Titus was a church leader on the island of Crete and was a coworker in the gospel alongside Paul (Titus 1:1-5). The churches on the island were very young, and heresy was seeping in. Those who had become believers didn't yet know enough to identify what was true and what was false. Paul exhorted Titus to teach the truth of the gospel and how it informs how we live. Right belief leads to right behavior with right intention.

Verse 3 contains a list of who we were before Christ.

> What behavior or character traits in this list remain a struggle for you? Confess them to the Lord and ask for the Spirit's help to overcome.

> Define these phrases from verse 5 in your own words:
> • "He saved us"—
>
> • "not by works of righteousness that we had done"—
>
> • "but according to his mercy"—
>
> • "through the washing of regeneration"—
>
> • "and renewal by the Holy Spirit"—

Right belief leads to right behavior with right intention.

Perhaps the most confusing phrase is "through the washing of regeneration." The *Holman Illustrated Bible Commentary* explains it this way: "Some interpreters have understood this as saying that baptism ('the washing') causes salvation, but in the context human deeds are clearly downplayed and the emphasis is on divine action and initiative. The washing described here is the spiritual cleansing that is symbolized outwardly by water baptism."[65]

In verses 1-2 and 8-11, Paul reminded Titus what our character and behavior should look like as believers. The motivation for this conduct is found in Titus 3:4-7. We lovingly obey God in response to the lavish love He expressed to us through the gift of Jesus Christ our Savior.

Read Titus 3:6-7 again. What new status or position do we have because of God's grace?

Look up the dictionary definition of *heir*.

Because we have been redeemed by Christ, we are adopted into God's family and have become His heirs. All that belongs to Jesus belongs to us—His place, His standing, and His right relationship with God. We have a taste of that inheritance now but will know our inheritance fully when we are in His presence for eternity.

As heirs, we aren't saved so we can have happy, easy lives but so that we may bring glory to God. We don't seek to be nice people or follow God because we hope He gives us the desires of our hearts. God isn't a tool for our purposes but a sovereign, powerful King intent on giving grace lavishly to His people for His glory.

BUILDING YOUR THEOLOGY: Summarize today's key truth in 1–2 sentences.

LIVING YOUR THEOLOGY: How does this truth affect the way you live your everyday life?

PRAY: Thank God for sending Jesus to pay for your sins. Thank Him for adopting you and making you His heir. Express your love and commitment to walk in obedience.

MEDITATE AND MEMORIZE: Ephesians 2:8-9

REPENT AND BELIEVE

How would you define *repentance*?

I ran on the cross-country team in college. (Don't be too impressed. The team needed another girl to compete, and desperate times called for desperate measures. My goal at every meet was not to finish last.)

We would often practice by running the trails in the undeveloped portion of our eighty acre college. This resulted in a few wildlife encounters, including a baby bear and a couple of snakes. My reaction was never, "Oh! How cute!" Instead, it was an almost robotic turn and sprint, my heart beating out of my chest.

My animal encounters provide an excellent example of what it means to repent—to change and go in a different direction. The Greek word for *repent* actually means "to change one's mind."[66] But the New Testament meaning has been shaped by several Old Testament words and passages that called for a return to God and a change of a person's whole course of life. We see this idea in 2 Chronicles 7:14 when the temple was consecrated to God, and in Jonah 3 when God gave Nineveh the chance to avoid certain destruction.

True repentance is a hard turn away from all that doesn't please God to point our lives toward Him.

Read Mark 1:14-15. What was Jesus' first sermon?

The call to repentance in Jesus' first sermon marks its importance in following Him. Repentance continues to be a theme throughout the New Testament.

True repentance is validated with right attitudes and actions, confessing sin and seeking to remove it from our lives.

Although confessing our sin to God is important, repentance takes it a step further. The Holy Spirit reveals our sin for what it is, we confess that sin, then turn from it, seeking to live God's way. This happens not out of duty but out of a desire to love and please God.

> Read Psalm 51:1-17. What did David ask God for after his life fell into a spiral of sin?

This is a psalm of repentance. David committed adultery and then murdered a man to cover it up. But in this psalm, David poured out his heart in repentance. If we learn nothing else from this psalm, it makes clear this truth: There's no sin that is so great that the blood of Jesus can't cover it. God's call is that we would repent and believe.

One thing we need to understand: Repentance is not a onetime action. We initially repent as part of our salvation response. However, salvation doesn't make us act perfectly. While we're living we will still commit sin, thus the need to repent. We don't repent in order to restore our salvation, because we never lose that; rather, we repent in order to restore our fellowship with God. So whether you've been a Christian for decades or are beginning that journey today, we all have a need to confess and repent.

> What do you need to confess and repent of today? Write your own version of a psalm of repentance below.

In conversion, we don't only repent of sin, we also believe in faith that Jesus is the Messiah who paid for our sin on the cross. Gregg Allison describes true saving faith as follows: "Faith that saves stands in contrast with bogus faith, which is mere intellectual understanding or assent."[67] As James 2:19 says, "Even the demons believe—and they shudder."

What is the difference between a demon's belief and a Christian's belief in God?

A demon may believe in God's existence, but a Christian believes God is her only hope and acts on that belief with full surrender. A Christian doesn't only believe that the truths of Scripture are true, she stakes her life on them.

Read Hebrews 11:1. What does this verse say about faith?

A Christian doesn't only believe that the truths of Scripture are true, she stakes her life on them.

As said in *The 99 Essential Doctrines*, "Biblical faith is not blind faith, for it rests on the historical life, death, and resurrection of Christ."[68]

Read Hebrews 11:8-19. Write a list of all the ways Abraham obeyed.

Abraham obeyed in each of these situations through faith. He trusted in God even though he couldn't see or understand what God was doing.

I love verses 13-16. Summarize these verses in your own words.

Do you think you would have had the faith to obey like Abraham did? Why or why not?

Read Romans 4:13-25. What saved Abraham? What does verse 24 say will save us?

Good deeds don't save us. Baptism doesn't save us. Walking down the church's aisle to go talk to the pastor doesn't save us. Saying a particular prayer with particular words doesn't save us. Our salvation comes through the work of the Holy Spirit in our hearts as we repent of our sins and place our faith in Jesus. Christ alone saves.

BUILDING YOUR THEOLOGY: Summarize today's key truth in 1–2 sentences.

LIVING YOUR THEOLOGY: How does this truth affect the way you live your everyday life?

PRAY: If you haven't yet made the decision to follow Jesus, take time now to confess your sin and place your faith in Him. Once you make that decision, reach out to someone doing this study with you to tell them you've decided to follow Jesus. If you're already a Christian, take a moment to consider your relationship with Jesus. If sin is in the way, repent of it and ask God to restore fellowship with you. Also take time to pray for someone you know who doesn't yet know Christ.

MEDITATE AND MEMORIZE: Hebrews 11:1

WE ARE JUSTIFIED THROUGH JESUS ALONE

Describe the character of a good judge.

A good judge always rules justly. He sentences the guilty to appropriate punishment and declares the innocent able to go free.

Read Romans 3:9-20. What did Paul say about all people?

Breaking God's Law puts us in opposition to Him. His perfect holiness requires that we be sinless if we want to be right with Him and stand in His presence. Yet this passage states that every person is guilty before God. Verses 11-18 are taken from biblical wisdom literature (mostly the Psalms) describing the wicked. But rather than this being about our enemies, Paul used these words to describe *us*: "There is no one righteous, not even one" (v. 10).

Do most people you know take sin seriously? Why or why not? Do you take sin seriously?

Have you ever had a hard time reconciling God's righteousness and justice with His mercy and grace? Do you think these are opposite concepts? Why or why not?

Sin is worthy of God's wrath because it is rebellion against Him. We are all sinners; thus, we are right recipients of God's wrath. Yet this wrath was poured out on Jesus at the cross. For all who are hidden in Christ, the wrath we deserved has been absorbed for good. Because God is just, He will only punish sin once, and that punishment was complete at the cross.

What condemns us according to verses 19-20?

Because God is just, He will only punish sin once, and that punishment was complete at the cross.

We know sin because we know God's good Law. He has given us the picture of righteous living, so, by default, we understand what rebellion is. I tend to give people a pass if they don't know the rules or norms of how something is done, but we don't get a pass.

Read Romans 1:18-20 and 2:12-16. What do these passages make clear about our guilt before God?

Since we are totally guilty before God, without excuse and without the power to justify ourselves, God took matters into His own hands.

Read Romans 3:21-26. Note the key phrases and explain in your own words the great saving work of God.

Paul explained that God did something new through Jesus. He made a way for the unrighteous to be forever righteous through Christ. The coming of Jesus fulfilled what the Law and prophets had been pointing to for ages. Jesus wasn't just the better temple sacrifice; He was the perfect atoning sacrifice to end all sacrifices. He took our place and bore the wrath of God toward sin. He redeemed us and paid the price for us. And His sacrifice covers all people—Jews and Gentiles. All are justified freely by His grace. All are welcome to come to Him. All can be made righteous. Not because we have anything in ourselves to make us righteous, but because of Jesus. If we believe in Jesus, we are made righteous in Him and declared righteous by God.

> **What do some people want to stand on to justify themselves?**

> **Read Romans 3:27-31. What did Paul say we are justified by?**

We have nothing—absolutely nothing—that we can boast about to give us *justification*. We can't be good enough or do enough good things. Our justification comes only through faith in Jesus.

The term *justified* would have been recognized as a legal term in biblical times pertaining to legal status. It is a declaration that justice has been served and right standing has been restored, once and for all.[69]

Some define the term *justified* as "just as if I'd never sinned." That's helpful, but it doesn't capture the full meaning. We certainly stand before God forgiven and clean, but being justified means more. Jerry Bridges and Bob Bevington state it like this:

We have been made righteous, declared righteous, and justified through Christ alone.

——

"But it wasn't enough for us to have a clean, but empty, ledger sheet. God also credits us with the perfect righteousness of Christ 'so that in him we might become the righteousness of God.' This happens the same way Jesus was made to be sin—by transfer. Just as God charged our sin to Christ, so he credits the perfect obedience of Jesus to all who trust in him. In what is often called the Great Exchange, God exchanges our sin for Christ's righteousness. As a result, all who have trusted in Christ as Savior stand before God not with a clean-but-empty ledger, but one filled with the very righteousness of Christ! ... There's an old play on the word justified: 'just-as-if-I'd never sinned.' But here's another way of saying it: 'just-as-if-I'd always obeyed.'"[70]

We don't have a righteousness of our own, nor can we gain one on merit, works, accomplishments, or anything else in this world. We have been made righteous, declared righteous, and justified through Christ alone.

BUILDING YOUR THEOLOGY: Summarize today's key truth in 1–2 sentences.

LIVING YOUR THEOLOGY: How does this truth affect the way you live your everyday life?

PRAY: Thank God for declaring you righteous through Jesus. Thank Jesus for providing the needed satisfaction for God's judgment so that you could have a right relationship with Him.

MEDITATE AND MEMORIZE: Romans 3:23-24

ADOPTION IS GOD'S DESIGN

A few short years ago in a small county courthouse, my family stood before a judge who asked, "Do you understand this adoption means you are responsible to support him financially, physically, emotionally, and spiritually? This is a legally binding commitment. He will be a rightful heir, equal in rights to any biological child."

We agreed and the judge slammed her gavel on the hardwood of her stand. Paperwork was signed and our son's name—and his future—was changed. Access to parents who will love him as long as they are breathing was changed. Adoption changed his life (and ours).

Adoption is at the heart of the gospel.

My son is a Wiley with every right, responsibility, and reward of our biological child. In the same way, God has adopted you into His family. He may not have changed your name, but He has certainly changed your future, your identity, and your status. He loves you with the love of a perfect Father. He disciplines you and provides for you as a parent provides for a child. He is a good Father.

> What benefits, rights, and responsibilities come with being someone's child?

> Circle the benefits, rights, and responsibilities above that are also in place for those who are children of God. Add any additional details below.

My children aren't just waiting on an inheritance. They enjoy the benefit of being in our family now. They have a fun life and are provided for now. They also currently have responsibilities as our children.

Sometimes we forget that the blessings of being in God's family apply now, not just in eternity. Our status as God's children affords us immediate and close access to Him. We don't have to slink into His presence; we can come boldly. We can talk with Him about our hurts, our joys, and our needs and know that He will help us (Heb. 4:16). We get to enjoy the family of God, our brothers and sisters in Christ, who walk alongside us to encourage us and pray for us. We get to rejoice with those who rejoice and weep with those who weep (Rom. 12:15; 1 Cor. 12:26).

We need to keep in mind that our adoption and the blessings that come with it had nothing to do with us.

> Read Galatians 4:1-7. How did our adoption take place? What was the resulting status change?

> How would the life of a son be different from the life of a slave?

Both a slave and a son would be under the jurisdiction of guardians who would teach, instruct, and discipline them, but their futures would definitely be different. We are not slaves, bossed around by an owner. We are children of God, blessed by His loving guidance and instruction. Our status as adopted children changes our access to Him.

Our adoption as sons and daughters also brings us a new identity and a new freedom. We are no longer bound by sin but have the power of the Holy Spirit to defeat temptation. This holy adoption changes us and calls us to live in a way that the world does not understand. This new life we live marks our adoption. It is the signed paperwork, the changing of our name and our future.

> Does being adopted into God's family mean we get to avoid hard times and suffering? Explain.

> Read John 16:33.

Jesus clearly tells us that a decision to follow Him will absolutely include suffering. We will be treated as Jesus was treated, and He suffered greatly on earth for God's kingdom. But in times of struggle, the blessings of our adoptive relationship, both what we enjoy now and the hope of what is to come, can be a source of joy and strength.

> Revisit Romans 8:14-17. What is the resulting emotion of a spirit of slavery to sin and death (v. 15)?

> What is the result of receiving the spirit of adoption?

Through our relationship with Christ, we are no longer ruled by fear, cowering in the darkness. Instead, we enjoy the secured place of God's adopted child.

Through our relationship with Christ, we are no longer ruled by fear, cowering in the darkness. Instead, we enjoy the secured place of God's adopted child. We are given intimate access as we await a glorious eternal life because of our adoption into the family of God.

No matter your family dynamic on earth, in Christ you are part of an eternal family with a Father who is always faithful. You belong. You are somebody. Churches aren't perfect, but they are filled with your brothers and sisters. When you are saved, you aren't just saved *from* sin and death. You are saved *to* something. You have abundant life as a child of God.

BUILDING YOUR THEOLOGY: Summarize today's key truth in 1–2 sentences.

LIVING YOUR THEOLOGY: How does this truth affect the way you live your everyday life?

PRAY: Thank God for adopting you into His family. Spend some time thanking Him for being the perfect Father and for all the ways that He parents you well. Don't be hesitant to bring your requests to God, even the things you may think are trivial. If it matters to you, it matters to Him.

MEDITATE AND MEMORIZE: Galatians 4:4-5

BECOMING MORE LIKE JESUS IS A PROCESS

Mature. Grow. Develop. These are synonyms for the big, churchy word *sanctification*.

Sanctification is the salvation process of knowing Christ and becoming more like Him. The word *sanctify* in Greek is actually derived from the same word group as *saint* and *holy*, and can be translated "to separate" or "set apart."[71] God is setting us apart for His purpose and use.

Sanctification embraces the concept of "already but not yet" that is so central to our story with the Lord. In other words, when we surrender to Christ, we are saved. As we grow in Christ, we are being saved. Then when we die or Jesus returns, we will be saved.

Gregg Allison describes three aspects of sanctification:

1. Positional—An immediate setting apart from sin and for God's purposes upon salvation.

2. Progressive—Ongoing process of becoming more like Jesus that will continue until death.

3. Perfected—Upon death, Christians become like Christ, complete in salvation, including their glorified bodies.[72]

The majority of Scripture about sanctification focuses on progressive sanctification, which starts at the beginning of our new life in Christ and ends with our physical life on earth. It's walking with Christ and seeking to live a life that honors Him. This is not a linear process but an upward process.

> **Read Philippians 1:6. What does this passage say about the sanctification process?**

God started the process and He will be the one to complete it. However, we don't sit back and do nothing while God works everything out. We are part of the process as we learn, grow, and obey.

Read the following passages and note the different instructions given to us about our upward growth in Christ.

Romans 6:1-4

Romans 12:1-2

Ephesians 4:17-24

Philippians 2:12-13

Colossians 3:1-10

Hebrews 12:1-2

Take a moment to review your responses. Then, in the space provided, write a summary paragraph of all you discovered.

These passages are just a small sampling of all the instructions in Scripture of what it means to grow in Christ. But from this sampling it's clear that we are to think differently, act differently, and speak differently than people who don't know Jesus. We are no longer to be enslaved to sin, no longer to be conformed to the world, no longer to hold onto sin that so easily entangles. We are to set aside those things, figuratively put on the new clothes of righteousness we have in Christ, and live victoriously. We are to point our thoughts and intentions toward Christ and His purposes.

Sanctification is a lifelong process. As some have said, the Christian life is not a sprint but a marathon. And we are to run our race with endurance, not giving in or giving up.

We need to realize that there will be temptations along the way to rest, to stop growing, and to quit.

> Read 1 Corinthians 3:1-2 and Hebrews 5:11-14. What did Paul and the writer of Hebrews say to Christians who were not progressing?

> Have you been through seasons where your spiritual growth was stagnant? What caused it? How did you finally move forward?

The Christian life is not a sprint but a marathon. And we are to run our race with endurance, not giving in or giving up.

We all walk through seasons of difficulty, questioning, and weariness. But we can't stay there. The goal of sanctification is simple: God wants us to be farther down the path in our spiritual journey than we were yesterday or a week ago or this time last year. He wants to make us more and more like Jesus.

> What are the things God will use to work out this progressive sanctification in our lives?

Only God can transform our hearts, but He will use the spiritual disciplines of reading of His Word, prayer, fasting, meditating on and memorizing Scripture, worship, and service to do it. Also, God didn't intend for us to run the Christian race by ourselves. Your church should be a large part of your story of sanctification. As Proverbs 27:17 says, "Iron sharpens iron, and one person sharpens another."

There's no insta-Christian button or fast track in the spiritual growth process. Remember, it's a marathon, a lifelong journey toward a single end. How's your journey going?

> On a separate sheet of paper, draw a line graph of your sanctification journey from your conversion to today. Label your graph with specific events or years as you see fit. Would you say that the trajectory of your spiritual life is upward growth? Explain. What needs to change for you to keep growing in Christ?

One day your journey will be over and you'll experience *glorification*, that perfected sanctification where you'll be face-to-face with Jesus. As that day approaches for all of us, may we be able to proclaim, as Paul did, "I have fought the good fight, I have finished the race, I have kept the faith" (2 Tim. 4:7). And when we see Jesus, He will respond with, "Well done!" (Matt. 25:23).

BUILDING YOUR THEOLOGY: Summarize today's key truth in 1–2 sentences.

LIVING YOUR THEOLOGY: How does this truth affect the way you live your everyday life?

PRAY: Thank God for His constant work in your life to sanctify you. Ask Him to show you ways you need to grow to be more like Jesus.

MEDITATE AND MEMORIZE: 1 Thessalonians 5:23

FURTHER STUDY: What other questions do you have about salvation?

RESOURCES

PREDESTINATION AND ELECTION

Verses to view: Matthew 11:28; John 3:18; 5:40; Romans 8:28-30; 9:11-13; 11:5-7; Ephesians 1:4-6; Revelation 13:7-8.

Predestination is God's sovereign determination of all that happens, most often used to describe God's predetermination of someone's destiny.[73]

Election centers on who will be saved. Scripture reveals that God chose His people before creation (Eph. 1:4), so the question isn't *if* God elects, but *how*. Here are three views:

CONDITIONAL ELECTION

Some say election is based on God's foreknowledge of a person's faith. In other words, election is conditional upon how someone chooses. God is omniscient, so He knows all things before they happen. Therefore, His choice to elect someone for salvation is based on His foreknowledge of that person's decision to place faith in Christ

UNCONDITIONAL ELECTION

Others say God chooses the elect unconditionally, completely apart from a person's choice, whether that choice be good or bad. Again, the all-knowing God simply chooses some to be saved through faith in Christ. This highlights God's sovereignty, but does so without us knowing or understanding why He chooses one over another.

CORPORATE ELECTION

One other view of election is that God chose a class of people—all those who would trust in Christ for salvation, or all those who are "in Christ." Individuals themselves are not the elect but God chooses a group. It's this group of believers who've been chosen to receive the promises and spiritual blessings that come through Jesus. It's argued that this view of election corresponds to the corporate election of the nation of Israel in the Old Testament.[74]

The biggest question surrounding election is defining the interaction between God's sovereignty and human will. Scholars have debated this issue for centuries without a solid consensus. Ultimately, here's where we can land with assurance, no matter how we view the details: Scripture teaches that God is sovereign over all things. Scripture also teaches that people must choose to repent and follow Jesus. God's sovereignty and human freedom can be held in tension.

ASSURANCE OF SALVATION

Another source of tension is the question of whether Christians can lose their salvation. Passages such as John 10:28-29 (believers cannot be snatched out of Jesus' or the Father's hand) and Ephesians 4:30 (believers are sealed for the day of redemption) argue for eternal security. While other passages, such as Jesus' parable of the sower (Matt. 13:1-23), speak of people who appear to be saved but falter and fall away from the faith. Hebrews 6:4-8 even talks about how "those who were once enlightened" (v. 4) fell away.

Here's where we will land: In Romans 8:38-39 Paul stated that nothing is able to separate us from the love of God that is in Christ Jesus, and Jude 24 says that God will keep us from stumbling and make us stand in His presence. God will keep those who have truly given their lives to Him. And those who have given their lives to Him will remain faithful. Hebrews says, "We have become participants in Christ if we hold firmly until the end" (3:14). As Pastor J. D. Greear put it, "It is true that 'once saved always saved;' but it is also true that 'once saved, forever following.'"[75]

For more information on these doctrines, see *50 Core Truths of the Christian Faith* by Gregg Allison.

FAQS

Is baptism necessary for salvation?
Baptism is the symbolic action of being buried with Christ and raised with Him in resurrection. It is a picture of the new life that we have in Christ. Some denominations believe baptism is necessary for salvation, basing their argument on Peter's call to "repent and be baptized" in Acts 2:38. However, Peter also told the family of Cornelius in Acts 10:43 to believe in Jesus and be forgiven. We also note from other passages that salvation takes place through no other name but Jesus and through no other process but believing in Him (John 3:16,36; 10:9; 14:6; Acts 4:12; Rom. 10:9). From the whole counsel of Scripture, baptism is seen as a necessary step of obedience after salvation but not a requirement to salvation.

Why do Christians keep asking for forgiveness after they are saved?
Our sin continues to offend and displease God even after we have been saved. We are not condemned for it because we have been declared righteous upon salvation. So sin does not break our relationship with God, but it does disrupt our close fellowship with Him. When we confess our sin and ask for forgiveness, our relationship is restored to full health with Him.

Why is faith without works dead (Jas. 2:17)? Does this mean salvation is based on works?
Read James 2:14-26. Works do not save us; only repenting of our sin and trusting in Jesus results in salvation. However, our right response to the grace we have been given are good works. Good works reveal what God has done in our hearts, so real faith always results in action. Works are the result of faith; faith is not the result of works.

GROUP TIME

OPEN

Begin your group time with the large group discussing the following questions:

What was the highlight of your week of study?

What was something new you learned this week?

How did this week's study challenge what you believe about salvation?

REVIEW AND DISCUSS

Break into smaller groups to complete this section. Use the following Scripture passages and questions to review what you learned in your personal Bible study on salvation.

Read Ephesians 2:8-9.
How would you explain salvation to someone who has never read Scripture or heard of Jesus?

What does it mean to be reconciled to God?

Read Mark 1:14-15.
Explain repentance. Why is it necessary for salvation?

Explain faith. Why is it necessary for salvation?

Read Romans 3:21-26.
What does it mean to be justified?

What do people sometimes stand on to try and justify themselves? Why is this futile?

Read Galatians 4:4-7.
How did our adoption take place? What is the resulting status change?

What benefits do we receive by being adopted by God?

Read Philippians 1:6.
Explain sanctification.

What is the current trajectory of your spiritual life? Are you growing or stagnant? Explain.

REFLECT AND APPLY

Spend a moment writing your answers to the following questions, then discuss with your small group.

What other questions about salvation did this week's study raise?

What is your main takeaway from this study on salvation?

Why does what you believe about salvation matter?

Who do you know that doesn't know Jesus? What will you do this week to help this person come to know Him?

CLOSE

You closed Session 3 Group Time by praying for people who didn't know Jesus and for boldness to share Christ with them. Today, give an update on your progress on sharing the gospel with those mentioned.

THE CHURCH

SESSION 7

THE CHURCH IS LED BY JESUS

How would you define the church? Who makes up the church? What does the church do? Jot down your thoughts below.

Mark Dever describes the church as "the body of people called by God's grace through faith in Christ to glorify him together by serving him in his world."[76] *Church* isn't just the word we use to describe the building we visit; church is both the local body of Christ that gathers there and the universal community God has designed for those who follow Him.

While some disagree on whether the church includes those who followed God before Jesus officially instated the church, we can all agree that God has been saving a people for Himself for all of time, and those people have been meeting together for the purpose of worshiping Him. The Septuagint translates the Hebrew word for *gather* as *ekklesiazo*, a Greek term meaning "to summon an assembly." This word is very similar to the noun used in the New Testament for *church, ekklesia*.[77]

Read the following verses and note what each passage reveals about the church.

Matthew 16:18

Acts 20:28

Ephesians 1:22-23

Colossians 1:18

Historically, the church has been identified with four key attributes. The church is:

- one (unified);
- holy (set apart);
- universal (also described as "catholic," which means universal, and is not a reference to the Roman Catholic Church);
- apostolic (started by the apostles and led by their writings regarding the function and form of the church as outlined in Scripture).[78]

As marriage is an example of the covenants God made with His people, Jesus covenants with His bride, the church.

In the passages you just read, we see a reflection of these attributes. In Matthew 16:18, Jesus clearly stated that the church isn't Peter's; the church is His. Even so, Peter, as an apostle, would be a foundational stone on which Jesus would build His church. The church has been purchased with Jesus' blood, and it is Jesus who leads her. It's Christ who unites us, making us a part of something universal. Jesus defines the priority of the church, and He is the reason we gather.

> Read Ephesians 5:22-33. According to this passage, how is the marriage covenant like the relationship between Jesus and the church?

As marriage is an example of the covenants God made with His people, Jesus covenants with His bride, the church. He has union with her, just as husband and wife are two who become one. In this way, the church—both as individual congregations and as the larger body of Christ—is hidden in Him in His life, death, burial, resurrection, and ascension. Through this union, all of God's blessings are communicated.

Think about it this way: you're a commoner who marries a prince. Suddenly, you are in the glamorous pictures as well. You have access to the crown jewels. The queen knows you. You, a commoner who had little merit on your own, have gained everything because of your relationship with your husband, the prince.

In light of what you read in Ephesians 5:22-33, what does it mean to submit? How is biblical submission different from the world's understanding of submission?

Right submission is a picture of reliance, assurance of provision, and promise that whatever is being submitted to is in your best interest.

How is a husband to love His wife? How has Jesus shown husbandly love to the church?

How is a wife to love her husband? How does this reveal how we should love Jesus as members of His church?

According to verse 32, what is the point of this passage?

The covenant between Jesus and His church is characterized by being one with Jesus, being led by Jesus, being loved by Jesus, and being provided for by Jesus.

The joining of the church to Christ is mysterious, but we know that Jesus is the head of the church, who is His bride. There's a wedding feast waiting for us when we see Him face-to-face. Our earthly titles of spouse, employee, or parent will cease, but we will eternally be God's people, the church.

The covenant between Jesus and His church is characterized by being one with Jesus, being led by Jesus, being loved by Jesus, and being provided for by Jesus.

If the church is led by Jesus, what does this mean for the everyday workings of our local church and how we interact and serve there?

The One who paid the penalty for our sin now leads us triumphantly. The pastor is not in charge, and neither are other church leaders.

> Often, we think very individually when it comes to obedience to Christ. How might we begin to think more about our corporate identity as the church?

We aren't just individuals who have been saved; we are a church who has been—and is being—saved. We are led by Jesus, committed to serving, encouraging, challenging, and sanctifying one another in truth. We are stewards of His grace and His work. We are centered on God and His Word and led by the Spirit. We have a responsibility for the care of those within our church.

> Why is it so important for a follower of Christ to be part of a local church? When it comes to your church, what are you thankful for?

BUILDING YOUR THEOLOGY: Summarize today's key truth in 1–2 sentences.

LIVING YOUR THEOLOGY: How does this truth affect the way you live your everyday life?

PRAY: Ask God to give you a great love for His church, both locally and globally. Spend time praying for your local church.

MEDITATE AND MEMORIZE: Colossians 1:18

DAY 2

THE CHURCH IS THE BODY OF CHRIST

When I was in college, I had a terrible car accident that probably should have taken my life. I ended up smashed between two trees with a bone sticking out of my ankle, a shattered wrist, a busted nose, and an extremely bruised ego. I got out of the car, not yet knowing the extent of my injuries, and when I tried to walk, I face-planted. I didn't realize that my leg, an integral part of my body for the task of walking, was no longer working as it should.

The Bible says that the church is the body of Christ, and every single person in it has a purpose. When one member isn't pulling his or her weight, the whole body suffers—or, in my case, the whole body face-plants hard on the ground.

> **Read 1 Corinthians 12:1-11. How did Paul show the clear distinction between what the work of the Spirit is and what it is not?**

One of the struggles Paul addressed in this letter was the unity of the church. Part of what was causing the division in the church was the use and abuse of spiritual gifts. As Paul began his address on spiritual gifts, He reminded the believers that the standard for evaluating the validity of the gifts was the lordship of Christ. If someone claimed to be exercising a gift but he or she was not also exalting Christ, that person was not in line with the work of the Spirit.

> **What are some ways gifts could be used today that are contrary to the way God intended? Explain.**

Review verses 4-6. What point was Paul trying to make with his different/same statements?

Paul wanted the church to understand that though we are gifted and shaped in different ways, we are united in belief and trust in the trinitarian God.

What does verse 7 say these gifts are to be used for?

The Spirit gifts believers for the edification—or building up—of the church. Gifts aren't for our own applause or for us to hoard and enjoy ourselves. They are to be used in the body of Christ to move the church forward.

List the gifts found in this passage. Compare this list with the list in Romans 12:6-8.

Do you know how God has spiritually gifted you? If so, how are you using your giftedness in the church?

All believers are spiritually gifted. If you don't know how you're gifted, there are ways you can know. Spiritual gifts tests can help, but they aren't the be-all and end-all to knowing. Observe how God is currently using you to accomplish His purpose. Seek the counsel of others. Sometimes others see things you can't. Pray and ask the Spirit to make your gifts clear to you. And don't let not knowing your spiritual gifts paralyze you. Serve faithfully and allow God to reveal them to you.

Read 1 Corinthians 12:12-31. What do these verses say about how we should view both our gifts and the gifts of others?

Division wasn't a foreign concept to the early church. Jews and Gentiles, slave and free—they'd lived with division all their lives. But Paul's words made it clear that society's disunity was not to characterize the church. If the individual parts of the body of Christ are not unified, the church can't fully love each other and the world. All members are ultimately under the headship of Jesus, who instructs each movement.

Gifts are great, but without love, they are useless.

What is the difference between unity and uniformity?

Unity doesn't mean that all members will agree on everything or are doing the same job. That's uniformity. A church can't function in that way. Can I throw in a sports analogy for you sports lovers? A football team can't win if every player is a quarterback. To win, the team needs different players with different skill sets who play different positions, but all with the same goal. The church is similar. We're one team made up of different people with different gifts pointing toward the same goal. We're one body made up of many parts. Not everyone is an eye or an ear, but all are important!

Read 1 Corinthians 13:1-3. What was Paul's point?

Gifts are great, but without love, they are useless.

When have you seen people use their gifts in a way not grounded in or motivated by love? What was the result? What did you learn?

How do you see people using their giftedness in your church? How is your church being the body of Christ in your area?

A note of caution: ministry will be hard and messy at times. Using your gifts won't always feel fun and may go unappreciated. But you don't minister for yourself or your own glory.

Every Sunday morning for a period of time after my accident, my friends literally carried me to the car, drove me to church, and carried me up two flights of stairs. They checked on me every day. Without any accolades or glory, they were the hands and feet of Jesus.

We are the body of Christ, called and gifted to accomplish the purpose of God. No one sits on the sidelines. Every believer is in the game.

BUILDING YOUR THEOLOGY: Summarize today's key truth in 1–2 sentences.

LIVING YOUR THEOLOGY: How does this truth affect the way you live your everyday life?

PRAY: Ask God to confirm your spiritual giftedness and how you need to be serving in the body of Christ. Pray He will help you resist temptation to make His good gifts about yourself.

MEDITATE AND MEMORIZE: 1 Corinthians 12:27

THE WORSHIP AND CHARACTER OF THE CHURCH

How would you define *worship*? List a few characteristics of worship or write out your own definition.

Often we think about worship as singing to God, and it is, but worship isn't only about music. Ultimately, God created all things for His glory. His creation offers Him praise and declares His greatness, no matter the outlet.

Worship is our response to all God is and has done.

How does that definition differ from the one you wrote earlier? How is it similar? Explain.

Let's dig a little deeper. We respond to things all day. Our phone buzzes with a text message. There's a red notification on our email app. Someone opens a door for us. The food we just put in our mouth is too hot. All of those things create immediate responses.

God's work in our lives and our world also calls for a response. We respond with honor to God. We praise Him for His greatness. We thank Him for His goodness. We worship Him. Certainly we are to do this as individuals in our personal walks with the Lord. In fact, you should view all that you do as a way to honor and worship the Lord. Your attitude, your character, your decisions, your actions, your work, your play—all these things should be acts of worship, giving God glory. It should be the same for the church.

Read Acts 2:42-47. What actions characterized the early church?

After the Spirit came at Pentecost, Peter preached a sermon and three thousand people responded to the gospel. This group of new believers, along with the apostles and other followers of Jesus, formed the first church. The Acts 2 passage you just read outlines how the church responded in worship to the goodness and glory of God in their lives. They studied the teaching of the apostles and spent time together eating and praying. They provided for the needs of others in the congregation through generous giving. They gave praise to God. This first church modeled for us the practices of a healthy church.

From this passage, what would you say are the characteristics of a healthy church?

What characterizes an unhealthy church?

Do you see marks of health in your church?

If there are unhealthy aspects, how might you be a part of the solution?

We need to remember that the church on earth is not perfect. It's full of people, and people are messy. We all bring our baggage and biases to the church, which can bring hurt sometimes. If you've been hurt by the church, I'm so sorry. I beg of you: don't give up on the church. That doesn't mean you have to stay in the local congregation that has hurt you or that you don't need to heal from very real injuries. (If any abuse or illegal activity has been involved, contact the authorities.) But the church, Jesus' bride, is meant to be a means of grace to God's people. His design is that you would be embedded in a community that can love and support you as you seek to follow Jesus.

The church has been my stability in both the most difficult times—like when my dad passed away—and in the most joyful times—like when we brought our babies home from the hospital. A healthy church should be that for you too.

Read the following verses. What should we be doing for each other in the church?

Romans 12:10

Galatians 5:13

Galatians 6:1-2

Ephesians 4:32

Philippians 2:3

1 Thessalonians 5:11

The church is a reconciling and redeeming people intent upon helping others follow Jesus well.

The church is a reconciling and redeeming people intent upon helping others follow Jesus well. May we love one another, pray for one another, confess our sin to one another, seek to restore one another, and serve one another as we fellowship together. These kinds of actions should mark us as the people of God.

Do you see these marks in your church? Are these actions true of you? If so, how? If not, why not?

A healthy church should also choose leaders who meet the qualifications set out in Scripture. (More about this can be found on the Resources page at the end of this week.)

It's always helpful to remember that church is not about me. It doesn't matter if I love the music or if some of the programs don't meet my needs. Don't get lost in your own agenda and desires. If you do, you'll soon find yourself disgruntled and part of what makes a church unhealthy. Keep your heart focused on Christ and your arms open wide to those around you.

A healthy church worships. It responds to the work and glory of God with praise, ministry, fellowship, and spiritual growth. It's marked by prayer. It reflects the love of Christ to each other and to the world.

Don't you want that to be the character of your church?

BUILDING YOUR THEOLOGY: Summarize today's key truth in 1–2 sentences.

LIVING YOUR THEOLOGY: How does this truth affect the way you live your everyday life?

PRAY: Thank God for your local church. Ask God to show you what you need to do to help your church be healthier. Take a moment to pray for the leaders of your church.

MEDITATE AND MEMORIZE: Hebrews 10:24-25

DAY 4

THE CHURCH IS AT WAR

As Christians, we are at war both individually and corporately. It doesn't always feel like war as we go about our everyday lives, which I think is probably just how Satan wants it. He also wants us to forget that the war has already been won. Jesus has sentenced sin, evil, and death to a known end.

There will be no more spiritual battles after Jesus returns. But today, the battle against the darkness still rages both inside and outside the church.

> Read the following passages and note Satan's tactics against those inside the church.
>
> Acts 20:28-31
>
> 2 Corinthians 11:3-4
>
> Revelation 2:10

Satan is a liar and a deceiver. He hates believers and hates the church. He will use whatever tactics needed to try and tear us down—false teaching, persecution, division, and so forth.

Outside the church, Satan continues to blind and mislead people so they don't believe the truth. We fight against those lies, pointing people to the truth of God's Word that leads to salvation.

Even though the war is won, we are still in a battle. And God has given us instructions on how to wage war against the enemy.

> Read Ephesians 6:10-20. Who is our battle against and not against (v. 12)?

Too often we lose sight of who or what we're really battling. Paul makes it clear that we aren't fighting flesh and blood. (Although, at times, we choose to wage war against each other.)

> When was a time you saw the church in conflict battling the wrong enemy? What were the consequences?

Because the enemy is spiritual, we have to battle with supernatural weaponry.

Paul said our enemy consists of all kinds of "evil, spiritual forces in the heavens" (v. 12). Because the enemy is spiritual, we have to battle with supernatural weaponry.

> Draw a picture of the armor of God, labeling each piece. Next to each label, write a short definition of how the piece of armor is used.

This armor might seem antiquated, but for the original readers of this letter, the imagery would have provided a direct tie to the God who fights for His people. Tony Merida says it this way:

"While Paul is certainly aware of Roman soldiers, and was maybe even looking at them at the time of writing, his language is more influenced by the majestic warfare imagery of the Old Testament, especially from Isaiah. The Old Testament often refers to God (and His Messiah) as a warrior and His people as 'troops' who are in need of God's strength."[79]

This armor has continued to be powerful for believers across the centuries as we partner together to stand against the darkness.

Putting on the belt of truth means accepting Scripture and choosing to follow it wholeheartedly. The armor on the chest (breastplate of righteousness) means not harboring and nurturing sin, submitting to Christ, and living according to His ways. Having feet sandaled with readiness for the gospel of peace means trusting in the promises of the gospel, being firmly rooted in the truth. The shield of faith fends off the arrows of the enemy, giving us the ability to resist temptation and choose to do what's right. The helmet of salvation protects our minds from doubt and discouragement, reminding us that our future is secure in Christ. The sword of the Spirit is the Word of God, to be used both offensively and defensively. The enemy cannot stand against the truth of God's Word (Matt. 4:1-11).

As God's people, we must choose to put on all the pieces of the armor He has provided. Without it, we can't possibly be an army of warriors who push back the darkness and help rescue those who don't yet know Jesus.

> Revisit verse 18a. What other tactic is listed that is not a particular piece of armor? How did Paul describe the importance and urgency of using this tactic?

> Read the following passages and note how important it is to be a praying church.

> Acts 4:23-31

> 2 Corinthians 1:8-11

> James 5:16

These passages show us the power of a praying church. When the early church prayed, God shook the house and the believers spoke with boldness. Paul told the Corinthian believers that their prayers had helped him make it through a time when he "despaired of life itself" (2 Cor. 1:8). And James assured us of the effectiveness of fervent praying (Jas. 5:16b). I know it's a cliché, but it is true: the church does its best work on its knees.

Would you say your church is a praying church? Why or why not? If not, what can you do to help make that happen?

The prayer life of the church is as strong as the prayer life of the people.

The church that prays can stand against the enemy. The church that prays will push back the darkness. We say a hearty "Amen!" to those statements. But we need to remember that *we* are the church. The prayer life of the church is as strong as the prayer life of the people.

The Word of God assures us that we are ultimately victorious in Christ. But while we walk this earth, we're still locked in a battle. So, church, armor up. Pray fervently. Stand firm.

BUILDING YOUR THEOLOGY: Summarize today's key truth in 1–2 sentences.

LIVING YOUR THEOLOGY: How does this truth affect the way you live your everyday life?

PRAY: Thank God for the ultimate victory He gives us in Christ. Ask Him to help you remember who the real enemy is and to fight with the supernatural weapons He provides.

MEDITATE AND MEMORIZE: Ephesians 6:12

THE CHURCH IS DISTINCTLY MISSIONAL

Read 1 Peter 2:9 and write it below.

This verse is a picture of the distinctness of God's people. We are set apart for His purposes, a royal priesthood, coheirs with Christ, with direct access to God. He has called us out of darkness and into light. We now have the blessing and responsibility of proclaiming His praises and sharing the light with those who don't know Him.

God's church is called to ministry and missions, meeting the needs of people. That includes meeting physical and spiritual needs—especially their need to hear the good news of Jesus.

Read Acts 11:19-26. Where did the people scatter after Stephen's stoning? Circle the location names on the map.

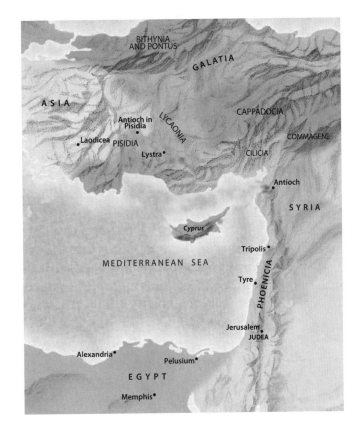

God used these scattered believers to share the good news of Jesus as they went, setting up churches all over the region.

Who did these believers tell first according to verse 19?

Although the Jews were the first to hear the good news, it wasn't long before God sent men from Cyprus and Cyrene to Antioch to share the gospel with the Gentiles.

Reread verse 21. Write it below. Underline what this verse reveals about the power of the Lord.

Throughout the Book of Acts, the power that fueled the missionary efforts didn't come from the apostles or the early church; it came from the Holy Spirit. The same Holy Spirit empowers the church today.

When the church in Jerusalem heard what was taking place in Antioch, they sent Barnabas to check it out. When he arrived and saw what was happening, he was overjoyed. He encouraged these new believers in their faith and brought Paul in to help disciple them.

This example from the early church resonates today. Everyone can be involved in what God is doing globally through missions. You can pray for missionaries and those to whom they are ministering. You can give to support the work. You can go. And you're to be doing the same things to support the mission of your church in the local community and surrounding areas.

How are you involved in missions on a global scale?

How are you involved in ministering to and sharing Christ with people in your local context—in your neighborhood, at your kids' school, at your job, or at the grocery store?

Read Acts 13:1-3. What does this passage reveal about the spiritual growth of the Antioch church?

There is no shortage of people who need to know about Jesus. But there is a great shortage of God's people getting out of their comfortable routines and being on mission.

Antioch had gone from receiving missionaries to sending them. The Antioch Christians were worshiping and fasting when the Holy Spirit instructed them to "set apart" Barnabas and Saul (Paul) for a special assignment (v. 2). The church was obedient to the Spirit's leading and, after praying, fasting, and laying hands on Barnabas and Saul, the church sent them out.

Read Matthew 28:19-20. What was the final instruction Jesus gave to the disciples before He ascended to heaven? Write it below in your own words.

This instruction still stands for the church today. As we go into the world, whether that's across the street or to the streets of Calcutta, we are to make disciples. We are to tell them about Jesus. That usually starts with sharing what Jesus has done for you.

Take a few minutes and write on a sheet of paper the story of what Jesus has done in your life. After you finish, ask God to give you the opportunity and boldness to share your story with someone this week.

There is no shortage of ministry needs or of people who need to know about Jesus. But there is a great shortage of God's people getting out of their comfortable houses and comfortable churches and comfortable routines and being on mission.

Would you say that your church is on mission? What is the evidence? Are you part of that evidence? If so, how? If not, why not?

Christ's mandate is for the church to be on mission. And you're the church. This isn't a spectator sport. Every member of the church is a minister. Every member is called to serve. Get to it.

List three people you know who do not know Jesus. Then list a few specific ideas on how you will to connect and build a relationship with them this week.

BUILDING YOUR THEOLOGY: Summarize today's key truth in 1–2 sentences.

LIVING YOUR THEOLOGY: How does this truth affect the way you live your everyday life?

PRAY: Pray for the three people you listed above. Pray they will be drawn to Christ, and you will have boldness to share your testimony with them.

MEDITATE AND MEMORIZE: Matthew 28:19-20

FURTHER STUDY: What other questions do you have about the church?

RESOURCES

CHURCH LEADERSHIP

LEADERSHIP QUALIFICATIONS

The Bible outlines the qualifications for two different positions of leadership in the church—pastor (also called overseer, bishop, or elder) and deacon. The qualifications for pastor are found in 1 Timothy 3:2-7 and Titus 1:6-9, and the qualifications for deacon are listed in 1 Timothy 3:8-12. It's interesting that the majority of the qualifications for both positions deal more with character than with duties. And the one significant difference in the two lists of qualifications is that pastors must be "able to teach" (1 Tim. 3:2). The pastor's ministry is to shepherd the flock and give spiritual oversight. The deacon's role is to serve the body of Christ. In Acts 6:1-6, a conflict arose between the Hellenistic Jews and the Hebraic Jews over the ministry to widows. Seven men, considered to be the first deacons, were selected to "to wait on tables" (v. 2). The Greek word used for "to wait on" or "to serve" is *diakoneo*, which can also be translated as "to minister."[80]

CHURCH ORDINANCES

There are two ordinances of the church: baptism and the Lord's Supper. Both of these ordinances were instituted by Jesus and are symbolic acts. When we practice them, Jesus' presence is with us. While both are a significant part of a believer's worship and practice, neither are required for salvation.

In both ordinances there is a pointing back and a pointing forward. In the Lord's Supper we point back to the Passover and to Jesus' last supper with His disciples, and we point forward to the marriage supper of the Lamb that will occur after Jesus returns.

In baptism, we point back to Jesus' death, burial, and resurrection, and we point forward to the promise that we will rise with Him when He returns.

BAPTISM

The act of baptism symbolizes the death, burial, and resurrection of Jesus that made our salvation possible. It also symbolizes that, by faith in Christ, a person has passed from death to life and has identified with Christ's death and resurrection (Rom. 6:3-5; Col. 2:12). Though symbolic, it is highly significant, giving the person being baptized the opportunity to publicly testify about the spiritual transformation that has taken place in his or her heart.

Differing views about baptism exist among Christians. It seems the pattern of the New Testament church is that baptism follows repentance of sin and trusting in the finished work of Christ on the cross.

THE LORD'S SUPPER

Jesus instituted the Lord's Supper (or Communion) at His last meal with His disciples as part of the Jewish Passover (Matt. 26:26-30; Mark 14:22-26; Luke 22:14-20). Jesus took unleavened bread and stated that it was symbolic of His body, and He took the fruit of the vine, which was symbolic of His blood. When we observe the Lord's Supper, we remember Jesus' sacrifice on the cross. There are differing views on the presence of Christ in the Lord's Supper.

- The Roman Catholic view: Transubstantiation. This view says the bread and wine actually become the body and blood of Christ.

- The Lutheran view: Consubstantiation. Christ is presents in, with, and under the bread received (as water in a sponge).

- The Memorial view: There is no special presence of Christ within the elements. The supper is a memorial to remind the church of the work of Christ on their behalf.

- The Spiritual Presence view: While the bread and wine are symbols, they are not empty symbols. Jesus is especially present spiritually when the supper is received.[81]

How often a church observes the Lord's Supper is up to that local church. The church also determines who can take the elements. Some churches limit it to only persons who are members of that specific church, while other churches open it to all baptized believers.

FAQS

Is it wrong to change churches?
There are a myriad of reasons why people change churches—worship style, preaching content, leadership change, and so forth. Some people change churches based on the needs of their family in particular seasons. Ultimately, the decision to change churches is between you and God. Of course, one clear reason to change is if the church you're attending is proclaiming and holding to doctrines that goes against Scripture.

One important thing to remember is that no church is perfect. Every church is led by—and is full of—sinful people. So mistakes will be made. Feelings will be hurt. Conflict will arise. It's part of being family. So don't be quick to jump churches just because things may be uncomfortable and you're not getting your way. Use the situations you face as opportunities to grow spiritually, to learn how to love people unconditionally, and to trust in Christ's leadership. Also, be careful about criticizing the church. One, you're talking about the body of Christ, and it's still God's plan to reach the world with the gospel. And two, you are the church.

Why are there so many denominations?
The rise of denominations began with the Reformation in the 16th century with the movement led by Martin Luther to reform the Roman Catholic Church. That movement gave rise to Protestantism, which since that time has broken off into several denominations—Lutheran, Methodist, Baptist, Pentecostal, and so forth. These groups worship the same God and proclaim Jesus as Messiah, Savior, and Lord, and agree that salvation is found in Him alone. However, they disagree on other secondary doctrinal issues that make it difficult to worship and do ministry together (infant baptism, beliefs on the Lord's Supper, appropriate church leadership, and so forth).

GROUP TIME

OPEN

Begin your group time with the large group discussing the following questions:

What was the highlight of your week of study?

What was something new you learned this week?

How did this week's study challenge what you believe about the church?

REVIEW AND DISCUSS

Break into smaller groups to complete this section. Use the following Scripture passages and questions to review what you learned in your personal Bible study on the church.

Read Colossians 1:18.
What does it mean for Jesus to be the head of the church?

Is Jesus the head of your church? Explain.

Read 1 Corinthians 12:27.
What does it mean for the church to be the body of Christ?

How are you gifted for service in the body of Christ?

Read Acts 2:42.
What are the characteristics of a healthy church?

Would you say your church is healthy? Why or why not?

Read Ephesians 6:13.
How does the church wage war against the enemy?

Are you a person of prayer? Are you a church of prayer? Explain.

Read 1 Peter 2:9.
What does it mean for the church to be on mission?

How is your church on mission?

REFLECT AND APPLY

Spend a moment writing your answers to the following questions, then discuss with your small group.

What other questions about the church did this week's study raise?

What is your main takeaway from this study on the church?

Why does what you believe about the church matter?

What is your prayer focus for your church?

CLOSE

Share the ways you see God at work in your church. Pray and thank God for how He is using your church to move His kingdom forward. Share areas of need for your church. Ask God to move powerfully to heal, restore, equip, and empower your church for ministry.

THE END TIMES

SESSION 8

DEATH IS NOT FINAL

Here we are—Session 8! I hope you have had many moments throughout these weeks where life transformation and true worship of the God who has ordered all of creation for all of time has taken place. Since the day God breathed life into Adam, history has been marching toward a very purposeful known end, or better said, a victorious eternity without end.

As humans, we long for happy endings, but we live with death as a constant reality. I shared earlier that when I was a child my dad was diagnosed with cancer, and he was told his time on earth was coming to a close. I saw a display of God's great kindness in giving my dad more time than the doctors anticipated, but still, I came face-to-face with his death in the middle of the night when I was eleven.

I remember poring over Scripture, seeking truths to cling to so I could grieve as one with hope.

Death came for my dad just as it will come for all of us.

Death isn't punishment for our individual sin but the result of a fallen world. It is outside of God's design but is to be expected and prepared for.

> Read Genesis 2:15-17; 3:19. What was the consequence of eating the fruit?

From the beginning, death was the result of living outside of God's intended design. A rebellion against the Giver of life resulted in a loss of life. We live under the curse of Adam in our fallen world, inheriting a nature inclined to sin.[82]

We all will face the moment when our bodies give out, our own resulting tragedy from the realities of sin. But there is hope! Death isn't final.

In fact, death is the completion of our union with Christ as we "suffer with him so that we may also be glorified with him" (Rom. 8:17).

Read 2 Corinthians 5:1-5. What do we "know" according to this passage? Write this truth in your own words.

While this "momentary light affliction" (v. 17) may cause pain, and even death, there's nothing this world can do to us that can strip us from the eternal promise of God.

In 2 Corinthians 4:16-18, Paul contrasted the suffering we experience now with the eternal glory we will experience in the presence of God forever. While this "momentary light affliction" (v. 17) may cause pain, and even death, there's nothing this world can do to us that can strip us from the eternal promise of God.

Do you fear death? Why or why not?

Read John 11:25-27. How does this conversation between Martha and Jesus calm fears you or others might have?

Everyone who trusts Jesus will not die in the sense of eternity. Although our physical bodies will die, our souls will be sustained and our bodies resurrected when Jesus returns. He is the resurrection and the life. (More about this on Day 3.)

Read 2 Corinthians 5:1 again. Paul used figurative language to talk about our current bodies and our heavenly ones. How did Paul describe our earthly bodies? The bodies that are to come?

What does it mean that we groan in our current bodies
(2 Cor. 5:2-4)?

While in these physical bodies, we experience suffering and affliction, but we know that will change when we take on our heavenly bodies.

What do you think Paul meant when he talked about us being "naked" (v. 3) and "unclothed" (v. 4)?

When we die, our spirits will be "unzipped" from our physical bodies. Our bodies will decompose, but our spirits will exist "unclothed" for a season, meaning we will not yet have our resurrected bodies. We will spiritually exist in what some call the "intermediate state."[83] We will not receive our resurrected, glorified bodies until Jesus returns. This disembodied existence isn't a state of unconsciousness (sleep) or purgatory, where God's people suffer so they can be purified to enter heaven; rather, during this intermediate time, we who know Christ will be in heaven with Him. Paul made that clear, stating that when we are "away from the body" we will be "at home with the Lord" (2 Cor. 5:8).

Read Luke 23:39-43. How does this passage verify Paul's claim?

Just like the thief on the cross who professed faith in Christ, at death, we will be with Jesus.

Then, when Jesus returns, we will receive our glorified, perfected bodies. This will be our eternal heavenly dwelling, swallowing up our mortality with eternal life. (More on our resurrection on Day 3.)

Read Luke 16:19-31. From this story, what can we discern happens to those who don't know Christ when they die?

Passages like this reveal that the believer and the unbeliever face two very different realities after death. The unbeliever will be in hell, and the believer will be with God in heaven.

Death is inevitable, but it isn't the end.

Death is inevitable, but it isn't the end. Of course, when we experience the death of a beloved family member or friend, we hurt. We grieve. Death leaves an emptiness. But if our loved one knows Christ, we can grieve with hope. We know where he or she is, and we know that some day we will be reunited.

For Christians, death means victory. It's the realization of what we've hoped and waited for. We don't have to fear death, because God has told us through His Word what happens after it:

> "The one who believes in me, even if he dies, will live."
> JOHN 11:25

BUILDING YOUR THEOLOGY: Summarize today's key truth in 1–2 sentences.

LIVING YOUR THEOLOGY: How does this truth affect the way you live your everyday life?

PRAY: Thank God He has made a way for you, that in Christ, even though you die, you will live. If you have fears about death, talk to God about them. Ask Him to calm your fears and help you rest in His promises.

MEDITATE AND MEMORIZE: Romans 8:38-39

THE PROMISED RETURN OF JESUS

A trumpet sounds. The ground trembles and graves burst open.
Our King rides in on a white horse to be lauded as the rightful
Victor over all the world. God's unveiled glory and power is
unleashed, and we will dwell with Him forever. It is finished.

Jesus' return isn't a crazy plot twist that no one saw coming.
It's a promise.

> Read Matthew 24:1-31. What are your thoughts and
> questions about this passage?

Much has been written about the timing and meaning of the events
mentioned in this passage. But Craig Blomberg says they "do not
necessarily prove that the end is coming immediately. Rather, they
characterize the entire interadvent period—what we often call the
church age," which will continue until Jesus returns.[84] Obviously,
events such as these have been happening since the Old Testament,
and this passage promises they will continue until Jesus returns.
Blomberg says the first nine events listed occurred before the
temple in Jerusalem was destroyed in AD 70. However, they also
have reoccurred since then. It seems they are a foretaste of what is
to come.[85]

The views on the timing and order of the end times events
surrounding Jesus' return are varied and sometimes strongly
debated. (See the Resources page at the end of this week for more
on these views.) But one thing every view agrees on is that Jesus will
return to earth one day.

> Review verses 9-14. What warnings and encouragement
> do you find in this passage?

Until Christ returns, hostility toward the gospel and those who carry it will not subside. People will continue to reject God and the good news of His kingdom. We should not be surprised. However, we are called to remain faithful regardless of what we face. And the good news is that the proclamation of the good news will not be thwarted. It will be told to all nations before the end of time.

Scholars again disagree on the timing and fulfillment of the great _tribulation_ discussed in verses 15-28. Some say this prophecy pertains to the time of the Roman siege and destruction of the temple in AD 70, while others place these events in the future still to come. Others choose a view that has both—these events have been fulfilled and will be again.

One thing to note: despite the great distress that is coming, God remains in charge. The world doesn't spin out of control. It does seem that there is coming a time when the press of evil will be almost unbearable. But it is not for us to fear. We can rest in God's promise that all who trust Jesus will remain in His keeping. If we experience this period of suffering, may we stay faithful, secure in the promises of God that Jesus will return and declare victory over sin, suffering, and death. If we don't experience this period, may we stay faithful, secure in the promises of God that Jesus will return and declare victory over sin, suffering, and death. Either way, don't fall away or despair. We serve the victorious One.

> Read Matthew 24:29-44. Write what each section of this passage says about the timing of Jesus' return.
>
> vv. 29-31
>
> vv. 32-35
>
> vv. 36-44

We don't know the particular date or time for Jesus' return, but we know that every day that passes means we're one day closer. I was a preteen when the calendar turned to the year 2000. People were making dire predictions that raised fear over what the new millennium would bring. Would Jesus return? Would the world explode? I fell prey to the fear. Yet this passage clearly states that anyone who claims to know the end of the world is incorrect. Only God knows when this will occur. Our responsibility is to be ready.

> Verse 42 says we should "be alert" since we don't know the exact time of Jesus' return. What does it look like to live life on alert?

> Read 2 Peter 3:9. Why hasn't Jesus returned yet?

God is kind and patient, continuing to give opportunities for those who aren't saved to repent and follow Him.

> How does this delay affect our preparedness?

Part of our preparation for Christ's coming is to help those who don't know Him to be ready. The joy of our security in Christ should move us to share the gospel with those who remain unprepared.

> Read Acts 1:9-11. How will Jesus return?

Jesus' second coming will be the realization of our victory, and He will return just as He went up into heaven. We will see Him coming on the clouds, and we will be gathered with Him in the sky!

I hold my views on end times, or what is formally called _eschatology_, loosely. We can be certain Jesus will return, but the order of events and happenings are less firm. I trust Jesus to work out all the details

The joy of our security in Christ should move us to share the gospel with those who remain unprepared.

and to keep His promise that we will be with Him. He will return and make all things new. A day is coming when even the sting of an early summer sunburn or the disappointment of a failure won't exist. Jesus is faithful to His promises, and He will return to rule and reign forever.

We have nothing to fear, for our King is coming.

> "He who testifies about these things says, 'Yes, I am coming soon.' Amen! Come, Lord Jesus!"
> REVELATION 22:20

BUILDING YOUR THEOLOGY: Summarize today's key truth in 1–2 sentences.

LIVING YOUR THEOLOGY: How does this truth affect the way you live your everyday life?

PRAY: Thank God that Jesus is coming again to reign and restore all things. Ask God to help you prepare your own life for His coming and share the gospel with those who are not yet ready.

MEDITATE AND MEMORIZE: Luke 12:40

DAY 3

OUR RESURRECTION IS COMING

As a child, I was so paralyzed by the fear that someone was going to break in and take my life during the night that I struggled to fall asleep. I would run to my parents with every sound I heard outside. I had to know the sound I heard wasn't a guy in a ski mask, so I often made my mom go outside with me to check.

I just wanted to know what was going on.

I still like being in the know. I want to know what's out there in the future. And although I don't know the details, God has given me enough of the plan to rest in Him. What is essential to believe about death and the end times is Jesus will return to restore all things. He will be victorious. He will reign and dwell with us forever! And we will be resurrected to live with Christ.

Essentially, all of 1 Corinthians 15 deals with the resurrection. We touched on a few verses from this chapter earlier in the study, but let's dig in a little deeper today.

> Read 1 Corinthians 15:1-19. Why does Paul dedicate this portion of his letter to the resurrection (vv. 1-2,12)?

It seems there was confusion in the Corinthian church about Jesus' resurrection. Some were saying it never happened. Paul wanted to make clear the certainty and importance of this event.

> Why did Paul say the resurrection was essential to the gospel (vv. 13-19)?

Do you think we have lost the awe of the resurrection in our world today? Why or why not?

Since Jesus did rise from the dead, we can trust the promise of our resurrection is guaranteed through Him.

What we believe about death and what happens after we die is in direct correlation with what we believe about Jesus, His resurrection, and His return. His resurrection is essential to the gospel message. If He didn't rise from the dead as He said He would, then why should we believe anything else He taught to be true?

Jesus' resurrection is essential to our faith because without it, our sin has not been forgiven; thus, we lack a right relationship with God. But since Jesus did rise from the dead, we can trust the promise of our resurrection is guaranteed through Him.

Read 1 Corinthians 15:20-28. What did Paul call Jesus in verse 20?

If you remember from our earlier discussion on firstfruits, the Jews celebrated the first part of the harvest as a guarantee of what was to come. Jesus was the first to be resurrected. There had been others brought back to life (like Lazarus in John 11:1-44), but they died again. Jesus was raised in a perfected, glorified body, unable to suffer or die. We will follow suit. We will be raised from the dead with glorified bodies when Jesus returns. This body will be our eternal dwelling. If Jesus returns before we die, we won't need to be raised, but we will be changed in an instant, caught up in the sky with Him.

Write verse 22 below. Circle the two names. Underline the action connected to each person.

Read 1 Corinthians 15:29-34.

The false teachers in the Corinthian church were denying the resurrection and encouraging sin, living as if there were no accountability. Paul exhorted the Corinthians to get it together and come to their senses (literally, "sober up").[86] They needed to put their faith where it belonged: in the only God who has the power to raise the dead.

Verse 29 references a practice of people being baptized for the dead. Scholars aren't sure how this practice was being used. It may have been for those who were converted but died before baptism. Paul wasn't endorsing this practice but simply pointing out how insane it was to participate in a practice that involved both death and resurrection if they believed there was no resurrection.

Read 1 Corinthians 15:35-49. What do verses 36-37 mean?

Paul lived in an agrarian culture, so the hearers of this letter would understand this analogy. A seed can't begin to grow until it splits open as it decomposes. Literally, life comes from death. When Jesus returns, our decomposed bodies will miraculously rearrange, and our bodies will be made new and perfect, resurrected to life forever.

Review verses 40-44. Fill in the chart to show the comparison Paul makes between the old body and the new body. I've given you an example.

OLD BODY	NEW BODY
Sown in corruption	Raised in incorruption

While Paul's description is meant to help us better understand the nature of the resurrection body, it is still beyond our comprehension. What we can know is that our earthly bodies will be transformed.

What two men are being compared and contrasted in verses 45-49? What is Paul's point?

Jesus lived the life Adam failed to live because He lived without sin and paid the penalty for our sin that we deserved. We bear the image of Adam and bear the consequence of his sin. But in Christ, we have been given abundant and eternal life. We will be raised to reign with Him as heirs of God.

Read 1 Corinthians 15:50-58. List the phrases you can cling to when fear or uncertainty about the future grips you.

The one thing people fear the most is death. But in Christ, you no longer have to fear. He has defeated death. He has been raised. And you will be too, to live with Him forever. Thanks be to God!

BUILDING YOUR THEOLOGY: How would you summarize today's key truth in 1–2 sentences?

LIVING YOUR THEOLOGY: How does this truth affect the way you live your everyday life?

PRAY: Thank God your resurrection and eternal life with Him are as sure as Jesus' resurrection.

MEDITATE AND MEMORIZE: 1 Corinthians 15:56-57

DAY 4

JUDGMENT IS CERTAIN

There is much speculation and uncertainty over what happens at the end—at the end of life and at the end of time.

> Read the following passages and write what we can know for certain about the end.
>
> Acts 17:31
>
> 2 Corinthians 5:10
>
> Hebrews 9:27

While there is still much mystery veiling what takes place in the end, one thing seems certain—all of us will stand before the judgment seat of Christ.

Scholars differ on the number of judgments and who will be at each judgment. But let's take a look at Scripture concerning the judgment and see what we can determine.

> Read Revelation 20:11-15. Describe this scene in your own words.

Wow! Quite the scene! God's power and justice are on display as He sits upon the throne. Verse 11 says it well—even earth and heaven fled from His powerful, awe-inspiring presence. The passage states that "the dead, the great and the small" (v. 12) are standing before this throne, and as they stand, books are opened.

> What did these books contain?

It seems the lives of the dead are judged "according to their works" (vv. 12,13) recorded in these books. One book in particular is named the book of life. All those whose names are not in this book are thrown into the lake of fire, referred to as the second death.

> Will Christians be judged based on the same criteria as those who don't know Christ? Explain.

We don't have to stand before the judgment wringing our hands and hoping for a favorable judgment. That favorable judgment has already been given to us based on our faith in Christ's finished work.

Those who have trusted Christ as Savior and Lord don't have to stand before the judgment wringing our hands and hoping for a favorable judgment. That favorable judgment has already been given to us based on our faith in Christ's finished work. At the moment of our conversion, our eternal destiny was sealed.

> How does Paul affirm this in Romans 8:1?

> If that's the case, then why will we stand before the judgment seat of Christ? Read 1 Corinthians 3:12-13 and 2 Corinthians 5:10 to answer this question.

There are some scholars who think that believers will not actually be at the great white throne judgment recorded in Revelation 20. They believe we will have already stood before Christ at a different judgment, not to determine our eternal destiny, but to measure the quality of our works—"gold, silver, costly stones, wood, hay, or straw" (1 Cor. 3:12).

Regardless of when the judgment for believers takes place, how will our works be tested, and what are the two possible outcomes (1 Cor. 3:14-15)?

On judgment day, the quality of our work as followers of Christ will be revealed by fire. This is not a punitive fire but one used to disclose true value and to determine the reward.

What do you think about the quality of your work and service you're currently doing for the Lord?

Does knowing the coming judgment will reveal the quality of your work affect how you approach it? Explain.

We don't want our service to Christ to be motivated by fear. However, it is good to be reminded that we will be held accountable for how we steward the gifts and opportunities He gives us for ministry.

We will be held accountable for how we steward the gifts and opportunities He gives us for ministry.

While we as believers can breathe a sigh of relief when we consider the judgment, that is not the case for those who don't know Jesus. One thing is clear from passages such as the great white throne judgment (Rev. 20:11-15), the rich man and Lazarus (Luke 16:19-31), and the sheep and the goats (Matt. 25:31-46)—there is a distinct separation of people. One group will enjoy the presence and blessings of God; the other will suffer the consequences of rejecting Him.

What would you say if a friend asked if her sin really mattered, and if it mattered how she lives her life?

Read Acts 17:30-31. How does this passage answer your friend's question? What is the call to all people in this passage?

Sin matters to a holy God. Judgment is coming. But He has made a way for all who turn in repentance and place their faith in Jesus.

Jesus will keep His promise to return and judge the living and the dead. When will this take place? We don't know. But until then, let us not grow weary or complacent just because our eternity is sure, but let us continue to serve the Lord and share the good news of Jesus as long as we have breath.

Who do you know that's not ready for the judgment day? What will you do this week to share the gospel with this person?

BUILDING YOUR THEOLOGY: Summarize today's key truth in 1–2 sentences.

LIVING YOUR THEOLOGY: How does this truth affect the way you live your everyday life?

PRAY: Thank God for your salvation in Jesus Christ that prepares you for judgment day. Ask God to give you boldness and opportunity to share the gospel this week with someone who is not prepared.

MEDITATE AND MEMORIZE: 2 Corinthians 5:10

RESTORATION OF HEAVEN AND EARTH IS COMING

Every great story has a great ending. Some are shocking, like *Romeo and Juliet* or *The Sixth Sense*, and some are sweet, like *Pride and Prejudice* and just about any romantic comedy. It seems God has coded our DNA to long for a happy ending.

The end of a story normally brings some closure and helps you understand parts of the story you might have missed or didn't fully understand in the moment.

God, in His goodness to us, has given us the end of the story. Reading all of Scripture in light of this certain end will help us better understand the whole story.

> Read Revelation 21–22.

When Jesus comes again He will make all things new. Sin and death will be no more, and the curse will be broken. Jesus will reign over all things, and God will dwell with humanity.

> **Why is there no temple in the new Jerusalem (21:22)?**

There is a new holy city, and there is no temple in it because God's presence will not be confined to just one building; it will permeate the whole city. The city's beauty will be beyond our comprehension as a bride adorned for her husband.

The new Jerusalem will be magnificent! I've not yet been to Jerusalem, although I do have high hopes of getting to go there one day. But today's Jerusalem would look like useless dirt compared to the glory of this new city. This is where we will live for all eternity.

The description of our eternal dwelling place doesn't match with what we normally get from movies and other fictional stories. We don't get a pair of angel wings. We don't inherit a specific cloud to sit on. We don't play a harp. That version of heaven is less than desirable for all but the most committed harp enthusiast. No, we will be in God's presence, and all will be right, just as it was in the garden before sin entered the world. We will worship God through all manner of activity, including work. Remember, work was not part of the curse. God assigned work to Adam before the fall (Gen. 2:15). The curse made work difficult, menial, and frustrating. But in the new earth, we will enjoy work without difficulty, corruption, or exhaustion.

In the new Jerusalem, basking in God's presence will be our new normal.

What is the source of light in this city (21:23)?

There is no sun or moon because God's glory illuminates it. In this city we will see His face (22:4). On earth no person was allowed to see God's face (1 Tim. 6:16). It was so glorious that people would die instantly if they gazed upon Him (Ex. 33:12-23). In the new Jerusalem, basking in God's presence will be our new normal.

Write the first phrase of Revelation 22:3 in the space below. What does this phrase mean to you?

These two final chapters of Revelation contain many great and wonderful phrases, but this one should bring such joy and relief to our hearts—"there will no longer be any curse." Century after century, the curse of sin has ravaged us. But no more. No more disasters. No more tragedies. No more cancer. No more poverty. No more lonely nights and heartbreaking days. No more divorce. No more suffering. No more abuse. No more pain. No more tears. No more. Our God lives among us, and all things have been made right. Hallelujah!

And as we noted on Day 2, Jesus' coming is imminent. Soon, the restoration of all things will be reality, and the time between now and then will feel like a vapor in light of eternity.

Yes, Lord Jesus, come. Be patient with us and with those who have yet to repent and believe, but also do not tarry. Come, Lord Jesus, and end the oppression of sin on the world and make all things new.

> What brokenness in yourself, in others, and in the world are you most aware of right now? How will those things change when Jesus returns?

If you're in a season that feels hopeless, know that something better is coming! But also, if you're in a season of triumph and excitement, know that something better is coming. In the meantime, keep running the race God has set before you with your eyes fixed on Jesus. In the end, we win. And the prize is better than anything we've ever experienced and anything we could imagine.

> Consider all the beautiful words, phrases, and promises found in Revelation 21–22. Spend some time journaling a response to this passage below.

Just remember, learning and growing in your faith doesn't stop with the end of this Bible study. This is a lifelong pursuit.

———

Wow. Here we are at the end of this study. We've examined some foundational truths, mined some deep things of the faith, and wrestled with thought-provoking passages. Hopefully you're more sure of what you believe and more in love with the God who created you. Just remember, learning and growing in your faith doesn't stop with the end of this Bible study. This is a lifelong pursuit. I'm praying for you as you continue this journey!

How will your life be different because of what you learned in this study?

BUILDING YOUR THEOLOGY: Summarize today's key truth in 1–2 sentences.

LIVING YOUR THEOLOGY: How does this truth affect the way you live your everyday life?

PRAY: Thank God for calling you to Himself and providing a way through Jesus for you to have a right relationship with Him. Thank God for being in total control of all things. Worship and praise Him for His great work now and into eternity.

MEDITATE AND MEMORIZE: Revelation 21:4-5

FURTHER STUDY: What other questions do you have about death or the end times?

RESOURCES

WHEN JESUS RETURNS

WHAT WE KNOW:

1. Jesus will return (Acts 1:11).
2. Our bodies will be resurrected and perfected, and our souls will be reunited with them (1 Cor. 15:50-53).
3. Final judgment will occur with Jesus as Judge (Acts 17:30-31; Rev. 20:11-15).
4. Jesus will reign and rule all the earth (Rev. 11:15).
5. Satan, sin, evil, and death will be banished forever (Rev. 20:7-10,14).
6. We will dwell with God forever (Rev. 21–22).
7. Because Jesus' return could be any moment, now is the time to tell others about Him, follow Him fervently, and prepare our hearts for that day (Matt. 24:36-42; 2 Pet. 3:8-14).

For centuries, scholars and theologians have debated the order and details of Jesus' return. One thing to remember: the ordering of events is not an essential belief. How you view the end times should not interrupt your unity with other believers or divide the local or universal church.

VIEWS ON THE END TIMES

Below are the four leading views about the order of end-times events. These views center on when the millennium, or Jesus' thousand-year reign, will occur (Rev. 20).

1. Amillenialism—Jesus will not have a literal thousand-year reign on the earth. The number mentioned in Revelation 20 is symbolic of the spiritual reign of Jesus in the church age that has already begun. At the end of this era, Jesus will return, and the final judgment and resurrection will occur. Then the permanent reign of Christ will be established along with the new heaven and the new earth.

2. Postmillenialism—Jesus will return after the millennial (not literal) reign, which began at the cross. This view holds that the gospel and church

are gaining progressively more influence, which will continue until Jesus returns. Resurrection of unbelievers and believers, judgment, and the establishment of a new heaven and new earth all occur at the same time after the millennium.

3. Historic premillenialism—After the church age will come a time of tribulation, which the church will experience at least in part. Then Jesus will return and reign alongside believers for one thousand years. (Some affirm this number is literal, while others say it is symbolic.) After the millennial reign, final judgment will occur and the new heaven and new earth will be established. (Some premillenialists believe the new heaven and new earth will be established during the millennial reign of Jesus instead of after the final judgment. This view is the most literal reading of Revelation 20.)

4. Pretribulational Premillenialism (or Dispensational Premillennialism)— Jesus will _rapture_ His people before the tribulation begins. After the tribulation, Jesus will return and reign for the millennium, similar to historic premillenialism.[87]

(This is only a brief overview. See *Systematic Theology* by Wayne Grudem and *50 Core Truths of the Christian Faith* by Gregg Allison for further study on this topic.)

Guard against becoming obsessed with studying the end times. Too much focus on this doctrine will keep you from growing and learning other life-giving truths about God.

FAQS

What happens when I die?

When we die, our spirits are separated from our bodies, and we will remain in this disembodied existence until the return of Christ. Where we go depends on our relationship with God. For believers, the Bible teaches that we are immediately in God's presence (Luke 23:39-43; 2 Cor. 5:1-8). For unbelievers, they will find themselves immediately in Hades, a place of torment absent of God. The following is scholar Robert Stein's comments about Hades from his commentary on Luke 16:19-31:

"In Greek thought this was the place of the dead, and in the LXX it was used to translate Sheol. In the OT it can mean the place of the dead or the place where the unrighteous dead go. It is contrasted with 'heaven' in Ps 139:8 and Amos 9:2. In the present context it refers to the place of the unrighteous dead in contrast to 'Abraham's side,' or the place of the righteous dead. It probably is a synonym here for Gehenna, or hell."[88]

The intermediate state of being disembodied continues until Jesus returns and our bodies are resurrected.

Will Christians be on earth for the tribulation? Will it last seven years?

Scholars disagree on when the tribulation will occur and if God's people will experience it or if they will have already been caught up to be with Jesus. There is also disagreement about whether the length of seven years is symbolic or literal.

Are we living in the end times?

Yes. It seems the New Testament writers considered themselves to be living in the last days with Christ's return imminent. Paul told the church in Rome, "The night is nearly over, and the day is near" (13:12). In Peter's first letter he stated, "The end of all things is near" (4:7). James told his readers, "The Lord's coming is near" (5:8). If they thought the end was close, how much more should we? It is a call for us to live our lives with a sense of urgency and preparedness.

GROUP TIME

OPEN
Begin your group time with the large group, discussing the following questions:

What was the highlight of your week of study?

What was something new you learned this week?

How did this week's study challenge what you believe about the end times?

REVIEW AND DISCUSS
Break into smaller groups to complete this section. Use the following Scripture passages and questions to review what you learned in your personal Bible study on the end times.

Read 2 Corinthians 5:1-8.
What happens when we die?

How do you feel about death? How has this week's study helped you?

Read Matthew 24:36-44.
What can we know for certain about Jesus' return?

What do you need to do to be ready for His return?

Read 1 Corinthians 15:12-20.
Why is the resurrection essential to the gospel?

How does the truth about the resurrection encourage or comfort you?

Read 2 Corinthians 5:9-10.
What is going to take place during the judgment?

What are some misconceptions you or those around you have about the judgment, heaven, and hell?

Read Revelation 21:1-4. If someone asked you, "What is heaven going to be like?" what would you say?

What are you most looking forward to about heaven? Why?

REFLECT AND APPLY

Spend a moment writing your answers to the following questions, then discuss with your small group.

What other questions about the end times did this week's study raise?

What is your main takeaway from this study on the end times?

Why does what you believe about the end times matter?

What do you need to do to get yourself and others ready for the return of Jesus?

CLOSE

Take a few moments to share together your most meaningful takeaways from this study. Share how your life has been changed by this time together. Close with prayer and commit to continue to pray for one another.

Glossary of Terms

Atonement
A doctrine that states that God has reconciled sinners to Himself through the sacrificial work of Jesus Christ. The concept of atonement is seen throughout all of Scripture, pointing to the death, burial, and resurrection of Jesus for the sins of the world.[89]

Context
To best understand the Scripture, we must read it in context, which includes understanding the historical setting of the passage, the type of literature, and the cultural influences of the day in which it was written. Context also includes recognizing how each passage fits in the whole story of Scripture.[90]

Covenant
Refers to God establishing a mutually binding relationship with humanity. God blesses His people through both conditional and unconditional covenants. Conditionally, God blesses humans as they obey. Unconditionally, God blesses humans regardless of their obedience.[91]

Eschatology
Refers to the biblical doctrine of last things—the end times—focusing on the return of Christ, the judgment, the resurrected body, the kingdom of heaven, and eternal destinations.[92]

General revelation
Describes how God reveals something about Himself through creation or nature. This is more general or indirect information about God. Also called natural revelation.[93]

Glorification
Refers to the last stage in the salvation process, which takes place at the return of Christ when a believer receives his or her resurrected body. At that point, the Christ follower gains complete conformity to the image of Christ.[94]

Henotheism
Worshiping one god without denying the existence of other gods.[95]

Heresy
Any teaching that is contrary to Scripture and orthodox doctrine.[96]

Hypostatic union
A term to describe the miraculous combining of full humanity and full divinity in Jesus Christ.[97]

Incarnation
The term that refers to the act of God the Son becoming human as Jesus.[98]

Justification
Act of God, based on Christ's death on the cross, in which a sinner is declared righteous by the transfer of Christ's righteousness.[99]

Omnipotence
Describes God's unlimited power.[100]

Omnipresence
Describes God's ability to be everywhere at the same time.[101]

Omniscience
Describes God's ability to know all things.[102]

Penal substitution
The view that Jesus bore the penalty of sin for humanity by dying on the cross. This action satisfied the wrath of God, thus providing redemption and forgiveness for those who place faith in Christ.[103]

Polytheism
Believing in or worship of more than one god.[104]

Propitiation
A sacrificial offering that turns away God's wrath toward sin. According to the New Testament, Jesus was that offering (or atoning sacrifice).[105]

Rapture
A future event connected to the return of Christ where God removes the church from the world instantaneously. The word comes from the Latin term *rapio*, which means to snatch away or carry off.[106]

Sanctification
The process of a Christian spiritually growing into the image of Christ. This gradual transformation takes place through the work of the Holy Spirit as the believer pursues holiness.[107]

Sovereign
Biblical teaching that God is all-powerful and rules and works according to His eternal purpose, even through events that seem to contradict and oppose His rule.[108]

Special revelation
The revelation of God given through supernatural means, mainly through the living Word—Jesus—and the written Word—Scripture. This revelation makes known a sinner's need for repentance and salvation.[109]

Spiritual disciplines
Practices that promote ongoing spiritual growth (Bible study, prayer, Scripture memory, fellowship with believers, and so forth).[110]

Transcendent
The quality of God that refers to Him being distinctly separate from creation, while at the same time remaining actively involved in it.[111]

Tribulation
When used in the context of the end times, it's usually spoken of as the "great tribulation," and refers to a time of great distress that ushers in the coming of Christ.[112]

Trinity
Term used to define God as an undivided unity expressed in the threefold nature of God the Father, God the Son, and God the Holy Spirit.[113]

Verbal plenary inspiration
The belief that every part of the Bible, as well as every word in the Bible, says exactly what God wanted said. He didn't dictate every word, but He sovereignly guided the whole process so that every word would be His.[114]

RECOMMENDED RESOURCES

Mary's Top 5 Recommendations:

- *50 Core Truths of the Christian Faith* by Gregg Allison
- *The 99 Essential Doctrines* by The Gospel Project (free digital download)
- *Can We Still Believe the Bible?* by Craig Blomberg
- *Delighting in the Trinity* by Michael Reeves
- *The Christ-Centered Exposition Commentary Series*

Other Resources:

- *A Theology for the Church* by Daniel Akin
- *Systematic Theology* by Wayne Grudem
- *Christian Theology* by Millard J. Erickson
- *Concise Theology* by J. I. Packer
- *Christian Beliefs* by Wayne Grudem
- *The Cross of Christ* by John Stott
- *The Doctrine of God* by John Frame
- *God the Trinity* by Malcolm B. Yarnell III
- *Created in God's Image* by Anthony Hoekema

- *The Cradle, the Cross, and the Crown* by Andreas J. Köstenberger
- *Holman Book of Biblical Charts, Maps, and Reconstructions* edited by Marsha Ellis Smith
- *The Story of Christianity* by Justo Gonzalez
- *A Survey of the Old Testament* by Andrew E. Hill and John H. Walton
- *The Expositor's Bible Commentary Series*
- *Holman Illustrated Bible Commentary* edited by E. Ray Clendenen and Jeremy Howard
- *The Crucified King* by Jeremy Treat
- *Spiritual Gifts* by Thomas Schreiner
- *The New American Commentary Series*

ENDNOTES

1. *Merriam Webster, s.v.* "theology," accessed October 9, 2019, https://www.merriam-webster.com/dictionary/theology.
2. Strong's G2315; https://biblehub.com/greek/2315.htm.
3. Thomas D. Lea and Hayne P. Griffin Jr, *1, 2 Timothy, Titus,* The New American Commentary, vol. 34 (Nashville, TN: B&H Publishing, 1992).
4. *Ibid.*
5. Andreas, L. Kostenberger, Scott Kellum, and Charles L. Quarles, *The Cradle, The Cross, and The Crown* (Nashville: B&H Academic, 2017), 736.
6. *Ibid.,* 727-733.
7. George H. Guthrie, *Hebrews,* NIV Application Commentary (Grand Rapids, MI: Zondervan, 2012), 156.
8. John Piper. "Pierced By the Word of God." DesiringGod.com. https://www.desiringgod.org/articles/pierced-by-the-word-of-god (accessed October 9. 2019).
9. Wayne Jackson. "The Holy Scriptures—Indestructable. ChristianCourier.com. https://www.christiancourier.com/articles/31-holy-scriptures-indestructible-the (accessed October 9, 2019).
10. George Herring, *Introduction to the History of Christianity* (New York, NY: NYU Press, 2006), 49.
11. Charles H. Spurgeon. "The Treasury of David." BibleStudyTools.com. https://www.biblestudytools.com/commentaries/treasury-of-david/psalms-1-1.html (accessed October 9, 2019).
12. Bartholomew Ashwood, *Heavenly Trade,* as quoted in Charles H. Spurgeon's *The Treasury of David.* https://www.biblestudytools.com/commentaries/treasury-of-david/psalms-1-2.html (accessed October 9, 2019).
13. David Platt, *Exalting Jesus In James* (Nashville, TN: B&H Publishing, 2014), 17.
14. Kay Arthur. "The Inductive Method of Bible Study: The Basics." BibleStudyTools.com. https://www.biblestudytools.com/bible-study/tips/the-inductive-method-of-bible-study-the-basics-11628183.html (accessed October 9, 2019).
15. Craig L. Blomberg, *Can We Still Believe the Bible? An Evangelical Engagement with Contemporary Questions* (Grand Rapids, MI: Brazos Press, 2014), 35.
16. *Ibid.,* 16-17.
17. Thomas HartwellHorne, *An Introduction to the Critical Study and Knowledge of the Holy Scriptures* (United Kingdom: Longman, Brown, Green, and Longmans, 1846), 70.
18. Andrew E. Hill and John H. Walton, *A Survey of the Old Testament* (Grand Rapids, MI: Zondervan, 2009), 92-93.
19. Gregg R. Allison, *50 Core Truths of the Christian Faith* (Grand Rapids, MI: Baker Books, 2018), 90.
20. E. Ray Clendenen and Jeremy Howard, eds., *Holman Illustrated Bible Commentary* (Nashville, TN: B&H Publishing, 2009), 715.
21. Gary V. Smith, *Isaiah 1–39,* The New American Commentary, vol. 15a (Nashville, TN: B&H Publishing, 2007), 285.
22. John Piper. "What Is God's Glory?" DesiringGod.com. https://www.desiringgod.org/interviews/what-is-gods-glory--2 (accessed October 9, 2019).
23. Tremper Longman and David Garland, *Genesis-Leviticus,* The Expositor's Bible Commentary, Revised (Grand Rapids, MI: Zondervan, 2008), 53.
24. Stanley Grenz, David Guretzki, and Cherith Nordling, *Pocket Dictionary of Theological Terms* (Downers Grove, IL: InterVarsity Press, 1998).
25. Ibid.
26. Hill and Walton, 62-63, 112.
27. Kenneth E. Bailey, *The Cross and the Prodigal: Luke 15 Through the Eyes of Middle Eastern Peasants.* (Downers Grove, IL: InterVarsity Press, 2005), 52-54, 59.
28. Michael Reeves, *Delighting in the Trinity* (Downers Grove, IL: InterVarsity Press, 2012), 24.
29. Wayne Grudem, *Systematic Theology* (Grand Rapids: Zondervan, 1994).
30. *Ibid.*
31. *Ibid.*
32. *Ibid.*
33. *Ibid.*
34. Daniel Akin, *A Theology for the Church* (Nashville, TN: B&H Publishing), 497.
35. *Ibid.*
36. Robert J. Miller, *Helping Jesus Fulfill Prophecy* (Cascade Books: Eugene, OR, 2016), 2.
37. Peter Stoner and Robert Newman. "THhe Christ of Prophecy." ScienceSpeaks.com. http://sciencespeaks.dstoner.net/Christ_of_Prophecy.html#c9 (accessed October 10, 2019).
38. Anthony Carter. "Jesus Christ: Our Prophet, Priest, and King." Ligonier.org. https://www.ligonier.org/blog/jesus-christ-our-prophet-priest-and-king/ (accessed October 10, 2019).
39. Jeremy Treat, *The Crucified King: Atonement and Kingdom in Biblical and Systematic Theology* (Grand Rapids, MI: Zondervan, 2014).
40. Gregg Allison, *Historical Theology: And Introduction to Christian Doctrine* (Grand Rapids, MI: Zondervan, 2011), 370.
41. *Ibid.,* 377.
42. Kevin Deyong. "Theological Primer: Hypostatic Union. TheGospelCoalition.org. thegospelcoalition.org/blogs/kevin-deyoung/theological-primer-hypostatic-union/ (accessed October 22, 2019).
43. Strong's G234; https://biblehub.com/greek/243.htm.
44. Strong's G3875; https://biblehub.com/greek/3875.htm.
45. Allison, *Historical Theology,* 435.
46. Grudem.
47. Thomas R. Schreiner, *1, 2 Peter, Jude,* The New American Commentary, vol. 37 (Nashville, TN: B&H Publishing, 2003) 307.
48. Ravi Zacharias, *The Grand Weaver: How God Shapes Us Through the Events of Our Lives* (Grand Rapids, MI: Zondervan, 2010), 187.
49. Strong's G1657; https://biblehub.com/greek/1657.htm.
50. Michael Horton. "Did Old Testament believers possess the Holy Spirit the same way as the New Testament believers?" Ligonier.ord. https://www.ligonier.org/learn/qas/did-old-testament-believers-possess-the-holy-spirit/ (accessed October 10. 2019).
51. Tim Challies. "Tongues! Signs! Wonders! An Interview with Dr. Sam Waldron." Challies.com. https://www.challies.com/interviews/tongues-signs-wonders-an-interview-with-dr-sam-waldron/ (accessed October 10, 2019).

52. J. D. Greear. "What Is Blasphemy Against the Holy Spirit?" JDGreear.com. https://jdgreear.com/blog/blasphemy-holy-spirit/ (accessed October 22, 2019).

53. R.C. Sproul. "Is there a difference between being baptized with the Holy Spirit and being filled with the Holy Spirit?" Ligonier.com. https://www.ligonier.org/learn/qas/there-difference-between-being-baptized-holy-spiri/ (accessed October 10, 2019).

54. *Ibid.*

55. Kevin DeYoung. "Three Surprising Ways to Grieve the Holy Spirit." The GospelCoalition.org. https://www.thegospelcoalition.org/blogs/kevin-deyoung/three-surprising-ways-to-grieve-the-holy-spirit/ (accessed October 10, 2019).

56. Anthony Hoekema, *Created in God's Image* (Grand Rapids, MI: Wm. B. Eerdmans Publishing Co., 1986), 13.

57. Strong's G4161; https://www.blueletterbible.org/lang/lexicon/lexicon.cfm?t=kjv&strongs=g4161.

58. Kenneth Matthews, *Genesis 1–11:26*, The New American Commentary, vol. 1a (Nashville, TN: B&H Publishing, 2011), 183-184.

59. Strong's H5828; https://www.blueletterbible.org/lang/lexicon/lexicon.cfm?t=kjv&strongs=h5828.

60. D. Michael Martin, *1, 2 Thessalonians*, The New American Commentary, vol. 33 (Nashville, TN: B&H Publishing, 2011).

61. "On Sexuality And Personal Identity." SBC.net. http://www.sbc.net/resolutions/2304/resolution-5--on-sexuality-and-personal-identity (accessed October 22, 2019).

62. Luke Gibbons. "12 Statistics About Pornography That Will Blow Your Mind." CharismaNews.com. https://www.charismanews.com/us/73208-15-statistics-about-the-church-and-pornography-that-will-blow-your-mind (accessed October 10, 2019).

63. Allison, *50 Core Truths of the Christian Faith*, 113.

64. Max Anders, *Galatians, Ephesians, Philippians, & Colossians*, Holman New Testament Commentary (Nashville, TN: B&H Publishing Group, 1999), 266.

65. Clendenen and Howard, 1333.

66. Strong's G3340; https://www.blueletterbible.org/lang/Lexicon/Lexicon.cfm?strongs=G3340&t=KJV.

67. *Ibid.*

68. The Gospel Project. "The Gospel Project's 99 Essential Doctrines." https://s3.amazonaws.com/media.cloversites.com/e1/e1cf7600-ae97-4932-acb5-b26923792f7f/documents/TGP_99_Essential_Doctrines.pdf (accessed October 10, 2019).

69. Frank Gaebelein, *Romans Through Galatians,* The Expositor's Bible Commentary, vol. 10 (Grand Rapids, MI: Zondervan, 1976).

70. Jerry Bridges and Bob Bevington, *The Bookends of the Christian Life* (Wheaton, IL: Crossway Books), 25-26, as quoted in https://ericgeiger.com/2014/10/just-never-sinned/.

71. Akin, 754.

72. Allison, *50 Core Truths of the Christian Faith*, 267.

73. *Ibid.*

74. Adapted from *The Gospel Project*, Winter 2014-15.

75. J. D. Greear, *Stop Asking Jesus Into Your Heart* (Nashville, TN: B&H Publishing, 2013), 88.

76. Akin, 768.

77. *Ibid.*, 768-769.

78. Allison, *50 Core Truths of the Christian Faith*, 284-286.

79. Tony Merida, *Exalting Jesus in Ephesians* (Nashville, TN: B&H Publishing Group, 2014), 172.

80. Strong's G1247; https://www.blueletterbible.org/lang/Lexicon/Lexicon.cfm?strongs=G1247&t=KJV.

81. Adapted from Grudem, 991-996; Allison, *50 Core Truths of the Christain Faith*, 332

82. "The Baptist Faith and Message." SBC.net. http://www.sbc.net/bfm2000/bfm2000.asp (accessed October 22, 2019).

83. Paul N. Benware, *Understanding End Times Prophecy: A Comprehensive Approach* (Chicago, IL: Moody Publishers, 2006).

84. Craig L. Blomberg, *Matthew,* The New American Commentary, vol. 22 (Nashville, TN: B&H Publishing, 2011).

85. Platt, 323.

86. *The CSB Study Bible* (Nashville, TN: Holman Bible Publishers, 2017), 1036.

87. "Eschatology: Four Views on the Millenium." BlueLetterBible.org. https://www.blueletterbible.org/faq/mill.cfm (accessed September 25, 2019).

88. Robert Stein, *Luke,* The New American Commentary, vol. 24 (Nashville, TN: B&H Publishing, 2011).

89. Chad Brand, Charles Draper, and Archie England, *Holman Illustrated Bible Dictionary* (Nashville, TN: Holman Bible Publishers, 2003).

90. Adapted from the following articles: https://zondervanacademic.com/blog/bible-context; https://www.esv.org/resources/esv-global-study-bible/how-to-read-and-understand-the-bible/; https://www.gty.org/library/sermons-library/90-55/proper-biblical-interpretation.

91. Grenz, Guretzki, and Nordling.

92. Brand, England, and Draper.

93. Grenz, Guretzki, and Nordling.

94. *Ibid.*

95. *Merriam Webster, s.v.* "henotheism," accessed October 9, 2019, https://www.merriam-webster.com/dictionary/henotheism

96. Grenz, Guretzki, and Nordling.

97. *Ibid.*

98. *Ibid.*

99. Brand, England, and Draper.

100. *Ibid.*

101. *Ibid.*

102. *Ibid.*

103. Grenz, Guretzki, and Nordling.

104. *Merriam Webster, s.v.* "polytheism," accessed October 9, 2019, https://www.merriam-webster.com/dictionary/polytheism

105. Grenz, Guretzki, and Nordling.

106. Brand, England, and Draper.

107. *Ibid.*

108. Brand, England, and Draper.

109. Grenz, Guretzki, and Nordling.

110. Don Whitney. "What Are Spiritual Disciplines?" DerisingGod.org. https://www.desiringgod.org/interviews/what-are-spiritual-disciplines (accessed October 15, 2019).

111. Grenz, Guretzki, and Nordling.

112. Brand, England, and Draper.

113. *Ibid.*

114. "What Is Meant by the Verbal Plenary Inspiration of Scripture?" BlueLetterBible.org. https://www.blueletterbible.org/Comm/stewart_don/faq/bible-authoritative-word/question3-verbal-plenary-inspiration-of-scripture.cfm (accessed October 15, 2019).

WHAT'S NEXT?
4 MORE STUDIES TO KEEP YOU IN THE WORD

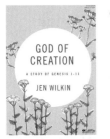

GOD OF CREATION
10 Sessions

Dive into the first 11 chapters of Genesis to revisit familiar stories and discover deeper meanings in the text.

LifeWay.com/GodOfCreation

GOD OF COVENANT
10 Sessions

Walk alongside the fathers of our faith in Genesis 12–50—Abraham, Isaac, Jacob, and Joseph—to discern Jesus in the stories of His people.

LifeWay.com/GodOfCovenant

DISCERNING THE VOICE OF GOD
7 Sessions

Discover the root to clear and daily communication with God—humble obedience.

LifeWay.com/DiscerningTheVoiceOfGod

THE QUEST
6 Sessions

Deepen your intimacy with God as you ask, discuss, and ponder questions of faith.

LifeWay.com/TheQuest

LifeWay | Women

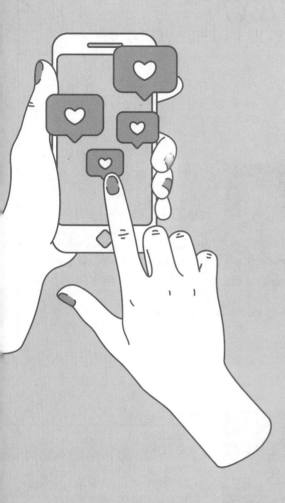

LET'S BE FRIENDS!

BLOG
We're here to help you grow in your faith, develop as a leader, and find encouragement as you go.

LifeWayWomen.com

SOCIAL
Find inspiration in the in-between moments of life.

@LifeWayWomen

NEWSLETTER
Be the first to hear about new studies, events, giveaways, and more by signing up.

LifeWay.com/WomensNews

LifeWay | **Women**